BACKGROUND TO ARCHAEOLOGY

Background to Archaeology

MARY CATHCART BORER

PELHAM BOOKS

First published in Great Britain by Pelham Books Ltd
52 Bedford Square, London, W.C.1
1975

ISBN 0 7207 0744 7

Printed in Great Britain by
Western Printing Services Ltd
Bristol

Contents

Contents

Introduction

Mankind as a genus has been in existence for a million to a million and a half years, and the species to which everyone in the world today belongs—Homo Sapiens—for perhaps fifty thousand years, yet only for the last five thousand years has he left written records of his activities.

Archaeology is the study of his early adventures in the world, his emergence from a primitive near-human to the creature we are ourselves, and the story has been put together from the material evidence he left behind him, his skull and bones, his tools and weapons, his pottery, his dwelling places and graves, monuments and places of worship—all the relics of ancient cultures and civilisations which have waxed and waned and for centuries lain buried and forgotten.

The evidence is sometimes slender. Often it is purely by chance that prehistoric remains have come to light. For a number of reasons, climatic, political and economic, certain parts of the world have been more carefully examined than others. Nevertheless, enough material has been collected to form solid theories which have been tested with all the logic and expertise of modern investigation and found acceptable. There are still countless questions to be answered, but new discoveries are being made all the time and a firm foundation of knowledge has accumulated, on which reasonable assumptions can fairly be made.

By the eighteenth century historians had come to realise the antiquity of man but it was not until after 1859, when Charles Darwin published his work *On the Origin of Species by Means of Natural Selection, The Preservation of Favoured Races in the Struggle for Life*, that the idea of evolutionary development began to gain acceptance.

At first Darwin's conclusions caused grave consternation

amongst people who had been taught that, in contrast to the rest of the animal kingdom, the human race was a divinely favoured creation, especially when he said that he was inclined to believe that education and environment produced only a small effect on the mind and that most of our qualities were innate. This was a challenge to the conception of free will and it was a long time before the theory was accepted by many members of the Orthodox Christian Church, even though Darwin's professor at Cambridge, writing many years later, said: "I stuck up for Darwin as well as I could ... declaring that he himself believed that he was exalting and not debasing our views of the Creator."

The knowledge of ancient man which has accumulated during the last century, as archaeologists have developed an increasingly scientific exploration into the past, has proved Darwin right on all points. He led the way to the discoveries of how and when things happen, although we still do not know precisely why they happened.

Climatic changes created conditions which gave nomadic food-gathering savages the chance to become barbarian agriculturists, and some of these barbarians founded the first civilisations of the world, with settled communities based on agriculture, practising the arts of pottery, metallurgy and writing, creating a social, religious and economic structure and living in cities. Yet these conditions occurred in many places and at many different times, and a civilisation did not inevitably arise on each occasion. So conservative is mankind, when he finds himself in a condition of life which is reasonably adapted to his needs, including those needs which he has created for himself, that development came about only when a small group of men and women, perhaps only one individual, of outstanding mental ability, had the intelligence, imagination and powers of observation to make use of all the advantages offered by his environment and create a civilisation.

Later civilisations came about, of course, by a diffusion of ideas. Elements of culture spread by friendly migrations and trade contacts and later still by conquests. Wherever and whenever these fusions occurred, they produced a cycle of change which seems in each case to have passed through the same phases, beginning with several centuries of quiet absorption, followed by the flowering of a new civilisation, and then a period of maturity, tending at times to stagnation, which lasted until the process was repeated by a new contact or by conquest.

The three stages of mankind, the nomadic food-gatherer, the agricultural barbarian and the civilised city-dweller, all had their cultures, for culture is a condition of thinking and creation which all men experience, whether they be civilised or not.

A record of man's activities lies buried under the ground across which he first roamed and later settled and in which he buried his dead. Throughout the centuries, layer after layer has accumulated.

It is a sobering thought that until the early nineteenth century there was no system of refuse collection and most people had no option but to bury their discarded possessions and household refuse in the ground surrounding their dwellings. Although most of the organic matter disappeared, such things as potsherds, which are almost indestructible, objects of stone and many bones survived. In medieval times, when a house fell into ruins or, as so often happened, was destroyed by fire, the ruins of the old place were usually levelled and a new building put up on the same site, with the new floor slightly higher than that of the original house.

Going back in time, the level of some of the Roman pavements of Londinium is seven metres below that of the pavements of the modern city of London. This must take into account changes in the water level of the Thames, which has risen since the first century A.D., but neverthless elsewhere in the city the Roman levels are nearly all at least three or four metres below today's street levels, which means that they lie below a thick layer of man-made earth and débris, which has accumulated in less than two thousand years.

In the Near East these accumulations are especially marked in the 'tells' or small hills, some of them fifteen or sixteen metres high or more, which have been created by people who have lived on the same site, building and re-building, for generation after generation, through thousands of years. By a careful excavation of these long-inhabited sites it is possible to distinguish the changing cultures and ways of life of succeeding generations of inhabitants, but it is easy to see what confusion would be caused and what wrong inferences could be drawn by an unsystematic excavation, in which the contents of the different layers became confused.

9

Introduction

The dating of the events in man's prehistory always presented a grave difficulty in the early days of archaeology, but modern methods are bringing an increasing precision to both chronology and absolute dating.

Geologists are able to determine the age of rocks by measuring the amount of radio-active decay, the rate of which is constant. Botanists have established a chronology for climatic and vegetation changes since the end of the Ice Age by measuring the thin layer of clay left behind in the melting waters of the retreating glaciers and by a study of pollens. For archaeologists the most valuable method of dating was discovered by Dr. Libby in 1949. This is based on the theory that, when organisms die, although part of the carbon content—C 12—remains constant, the C 14 content disintegrates at a constant and measurable rate. The age of the object can therefore be calculated by measuring the amount of C 14 still remaining. There is a margin of error due to random loss of disintegrating atoms and possible contamination, but the dates for the last forty or fifty thousand years can be calculated to an extremely useful approximation of about two hundred years.

This has helped immeasurably in correlating the labours of all archaeologists, from the patient collectors of potsherds and simple flint implements to those who have had the good fortune to work amongst the relics of the great civilisations of the Eastern Mediterranean, the Near East, India, China and Central America.

The story of prehistory that has already unfolded shows that mankind has shared a common cultural development, irrespective of race, for the characteristics of the three main races of the world, the white, yellow and black, have come about only through physical segregation in particular geographical environments. In the twentieth century physical segregation and isolation are rapidly disappearing and the lessons of the past indicate that the future holds a continuity of the process of integration which, despite frequent setbacks, has never ceased from the beginning of a reasoning mankind.

CHAPTER ONE

The Ice Age and the Beginning of the Old Stone Age

In terms of geological time, mankind's arrival on the earth, although the result of millions of years of evolution, is astonishingly recent, for the earth itself is of an age that the human mind can barely comprehend, the estimates varying between three thousand and five thousand million years: and probably the first five-sixths of this time was occupied by the Azoic or Lifeless Era. This was followed by the Palaeozoic Age—the Era of Ancient Life—a span of some three hundred million years, when the world was populated with sea worms, molluscs, jelly fish, trilobites and the like, culminating in sea scorpions and the first fishes, while the early vegetation of mosses and lichens developed into giant ferns as tall as forest trees.

The Mesozoic Age—the Era of Middle Life, which lasted for a hundred and fifty million years, was the age of the giant reptiles, and saw the first flying reptiles, which became birds, and the first warm-blooded creatures—the mammals.

The fourth geological era, the Tertiary or Cainozoic, is known as the Age of Recent Life, since its fossils show an increasing resemblance to modern plants and animals. Birds and beasts multiplied so prolifically both in form and numbers that this became the Age of Mammals.

As early as Mesozoic times a separate branch of mammals—the primates—had already separated from the main stem and were dividing into two distinct branches, the lemurs and tarsiers. In early Tertiary times there developed from the tarsiers two types of monkeys, the American monkey and the Euro-Asian

11

monkey, and before this dawn period had ended there had branched off from the Euro-Asian monkeys the important family of anthropoid apes.

Later the gibbons branched off from the anthropoids and later still the gorillas. Towards the end of the Tertiary period, when the climate was appreciably cooler, the orang-utans and then the chimpanzees branched off from the gorilla family.

Other forms of anthropoids were undoubtedly evolving during Tertiary times, one of which was to develop into a human being.

The fifth geological era is known as the Quaternary and is the time in which we are now living. It began less than a million years ago and so far is divided into two periods, the Pleistocene, during which the ice age occurred, and the Recent or Holocene, of the last ten thousand years, when there has been a general melting of the ice and the existing climatic conditions of the world have stabilised, with the world inhabited by the plants, animals and human races which we know today.

As the Ice Age approached, the whole of the northern part of the world was slowly rising. Though the southern lands of South America, Australia and South Africa were affected less, there is evidence that they, too, suffered changes through the increasing cold. In the mountains of South America, New Zealand and Australia glaciers which hitherto had remained high above the snowline crept down to the plains and valleys. Large parts of Asia lay under sheets of ice and even in the higher mountain regions of the tropics there were glaciers and sheets of ice which had never been there before and have never appeared since, while Antarctica, it seems fairly certain, was much as it is today—a land of snow and ice.

The Ice Age was not one long period of continuing arctic conditions. There were several warmer periods between the ages of intense cold. More than fifteen major fluctuations have been observed but the four main ice periods are distinguishable, named after the small rivers in the Alps where traces of glacial conditions were first recorded.

The earliest glaciation, the Günz, beginning about a million years ago, reached its maximum intensity some six hundred thousand years ago, and lasted for a hundred thousand years. This was followed by the first interglacial period of another hundred thousand years, which gave way to the second glacial period—the Mindel. This was the shortest but most intense period of cold, existing for about forty thousand years before the approach of the second interglacial—known as the great interglacial, for it lasted for some two hundred thousand years before the third Riss glacial descended on the world, lasting for forty thousand years. The third interglacial period was a long stretch of a hundred thousand years and then, some eighty thousand years ago, came the fourth or Würm glacial period which lasted for about sixty thousand years. The late Würm period carbon dating is from 12,000 B.C. to 8000 B.C.

The present Holocene period in which we are living may, of course, be a fourth interglacial period, for it began only ten thousand years ago. The ice is still retreating, but there is no knowing whether it may not return in a few thousand years' time.

In the northern hemisphere the ice sheets radiated from three main centres during the major periods of ice, eastern Canada, around Hudson Bay, in northern Europe and in central Siberia.

In Europe the ice crept from Norway and Sweden over the lowlands of Russia to the Urals, south to the Carpathians and the Balkans and westwards to the plains of Denmark, Germany, Holland, Belgium and France. Over the North Sea it met the sheets of ice descending from the mountains of Britain. The Rhine valley was filled by a mighty glacier and traces of glaciation have been found in the Pyrenees, the Caucasus and the foothills of the Himalayas, while the plain of Italy and the plateau of Spain were bitterly cold.

Even after the melting of the ice of the last glaciation there were several marked cold periods and in France conditions became almost glacial again for a time.

In the tropics and subtropics where the ice did not reach there were periods of heavy rain during the glacial periods, followed by drier periods during the interglacial: and these were sufficiently marked to change the physical environment, causing widespread changes in vegetation which affected the animal life and also the dawning human life, for it was during the Ice Age that man himself emerged, the product of a period of profound physical changes throughout the world.

At the first onset of the ice, the land connexions of the world were very different from today. The west coast of North Africa was joined to Spain at Gibraltar. Another land bridge joined Italy to Sicily, Algeria and Tunis. There were no islands of

Greece. Instead, a solid mass of land stretched from Turkey to Yugoslavia. The English Channel and the North Sea were still dry land and the British Isles formed the north-west corner of Europe.

The climate was warm at the end of Tertiary times and throughout the plain of Europe grew warm, temperate vegetation inhabited by rhinoceroses, mastodons, tigers, gazelle and antelope. Hippopotamuses basked in the Thames mud and along the shores of the Mediterranean grew palms and bamboos. In North America huge bison and mammoths roamed the prairies and the remains of an elephant nearly five metres high have been found.

With the arrival of the first ice the animals moved slowly southwards and the tropical vegetation faded, giving place to the hardier willows, pines, larches, oaks, beeches and poplars, and even with the return of the warmth of the first interglacial period, many of these plants and animals did not move north again, while some of the giant forms of still-existing mammal groups—the great marsupials, gigantic deer, mammoths and mastodons—began to fade out of existence.

As the first interglacial period came to a close the southern part of Europe was rising. Sicily, Malta, Cyprus and Crete were all connected with the mainland, enabling the mammals of Asia and Africa to wander into Europe. African mammoths, including the straight-tusked elephant and the lion, were at this time finding their way northwards, although the mastodon, the ancestor of the elephant, had by now become extinct.

It was in this world that the first near-human beings came into existence. In early Pleistocene levels in south and east Africa have been found the fossil bones of a sub-human race which have been called Australopithecines. The skulls have many human characteristics, although the brain capacities range from only 450 cc to 700 cc, compared with the 1500 cc of modern man and the 685 cc of the largest known gorilla cranium.

The limbs and pelvic bones of Australopithecus make it fairly certain that he walked on two legs in an upright position. He was a food-gatherer and cave-dweller, living on nuts and wild berries, and possibly hunting small animals, such as hares and moles. He may have used natural objects as primitive tools, as apes sometimes do, but he was not yet a creator of tools and therefore must be regarded not as a man but a man-ape.

In middle Pleistocene times another group of near-humans was living in the East Indies. In 1891, at Trinil, in Java, were discovered the thigh bone, three teeth and the top of the skull of Pithecanthropus Erectus—the ape-man who stood upright.

The thigh bone suggests that he was upright, walking with ease on his legs and thus freeing his hands for manual skills. It is more like a human thigh bone than that of an ape, and from its length his height has been estimated at about 1.70 metres. The brain capacity was 940 cc., considerably greater than that of Australopithecus, though still small in comparison with a modern human skull. It is not certain whether he was a descendant of the more primitive Australopithecus or another off-shoot from the human stem which took the wrong turning in the course of evolution and came to a dead end, nor is it possible to tell whether he had acquired the power of speech, although the parts of the brain which control speech show signs that they were beginning to develop. He had a small capacity for memory, but although he was able to profit by experience to a greater extent than the anthropoids, his intelligence was far below that of the most primitive races in existence today, such as the Australian aborigines and the Veddas of Ceylon. The teeth were very large and ape-like, and he had a receding jaw.

He cannot be regarded as an ancestor of the human race, but as a branch of the stem from which modern man has developed.

Other members of his family have been discovered in Java, while near Pekin the remains of forty cave-dwellers have come to light; they were similar to Pithecanthropus Erectus, although of a slightly later date. Their brains were considerably larger and the cranial capacity was 1000 cc in some cases. Neither Australopithecus nor Pithecanthropus Erectus left any evidence of having possessed a material culture, but the Pekin people had made a beginning. They fashioned crude stone inplements from greenstone, chert and quartzite, which could have been used for chipping and scraping, and they had learnt to make fire. They seem to have lived on wild game, though they had only the most elementary weapons with which to capture and kill their prey. There is a possibility, of course, that they might have used wooden spears with fire-hardened tips or elementary game traps, for the bones of deer, elephants, rhinoceroses, bison, water buffalo, camels, wild boar, roebucks, antelopes and sheep as well as sabre-toothed tigers, leopards, cave bears and hyenas have all been found near their dwelling places, many of them buried in the ashes of their fires, and it is difficult otherwise to see how they could have mastered them. There is no evidence of any formal human burial ceremonies in their caves, but some of the animal bones have been split to extract the marrow and amongst the débris they accumulated have been found human bones, similarly split, which suggests that they were cannibals as well as avid eaters of animal flesh.

Yet primitive as these people were, they were not necessarily the first tool-makers of the world. In Europe Heidelberg man was living, the first known European to come to light, having left behind a lower jaw bone, found close to the remains of elephants, rhinoceroses and hippopotamuses. It was found in the first interglacial sands at Mauer, near Heidelberg, Germany, and this discovery suggests that the pithecanthropus type ranged far beyond Asia. Like the jaw bones of the men of Java and Pekin, the heavy lower jaw of the Heidelberg man was chinless, but the teeth show human characteristics.

The ice and snow of the second and severest phase of the Ice Age began slowly to creep over Europe and America. Over the plains of eastern France the glaciers spread. The Pyrenees were covered with ice and snow. Scandinavian and British ice sheets joined and swept southwards over central and eastern Europe. Then, after some forty thousand years, came the warmth of the second interglacial period, beginning with periods of heavy rain. In Europe grew fir, spruce, maple, willow, yew, elm, beech, mountain ash, oak, poplar, lime and maple trees, with vines, clematis and fig trees in the south, and many of the mammals returned, including hippopotamuses, rhinoceroses, the straight-tusked elephants and lions.

In addition to the near-human types who by now were living in Europe, Asia and Africa, it seems probable that in Africa, mainly south of the equator, there were also in existence several possible developments in the chain of human evolution. The parts of a human female skull found in second interglacial gravels near Swanscombe in Kent are not complete enough to establish how far advanced in evolution this woman had become, and although in many ways they resemble a modern skull they are much thicker.

So far, apart from the rudimentary artefacts found with Pekin man, no tools have been found in association with these early

16

near-humans, but in both Europe and Africa tools have been found which must have been made as early as the first inter-glacial period. In south-eastern England flints dated to as early as the late Tertiary are considered by some archaeologists to have been man-made and used for cutting, scraping skins, boring holes or chopping, but these 'eoliths' are crudely chipped flints which may well have been produced solely by natural forces, worn into useful shapes by the action of the sea, by wind and rain, or the contraction and expansion brought about by alternating periods of heat and cold, and there is no real evidence that they were deliberately manufactured. Of the later tools, of the first interglacial period, no traces have yet been found of their creators.

The earliest human or near-human being to make implements and die near his handiwork was found in early Pleistocene lake deposits at Kanem, Kavirondo, in Kenya. This making of an implement for a specific purpose, as opposed to using some natural object as a tool, was a vital step forward in the development of man from the primates, for although some of the great apes show extraordinary dexterity in using tools provided for them they do not have the ability to create them.

Before he took to using flint or stone as an artefact, man must in all probability have used wood, as chimpanzees do to reach fruit and similar food which is beyond their normal reach, but the only wooden implement to have escaped decay yet found in early Pleistocene levels is a sharply pointed wooden spearhead, discovered in England, in a peaty deposit at Clacton-on-Sea. Bone would have proved useful for obtaining the wood, but once men had discovered the value of flint and the relative ease with which it can be chipped and flaked to form a useful cutting edge, they tended to use it almost exclusively for thousands of years to come. This essential conservatism is, as we shall see, characteristic of most human beings throughout all stages of civilisation.

From this stage when man began to shape stone and flint for his needs and left these archaeological records—the tangible results of his activities—alongside his mortal remains, time can be recorded in more detail, divided into periods which correspond to his progress.

He was not particularly inventive in the early stages of his existence and disliked change, which came about only very slowly, and even then usually through the stimulus of an encounter with some other group. He lived in places where he could most easily obtain the materials he wanted in order to secure his food—the first necessity of all living creatures—and for the first two hundred thousand years of his existence his principal requirements were stone and flint for his hunting and food-gathering.

This, in archaeological terms, is the Lower Palaeolithic or earliest part of the Old Stone Age, and apart from the doubtful period of the eoliths two cultures are discernible, the Abbevillian of the first interglacial and the Acheulean of the second interglacial. The terms are arbitrary, named after the places where they were first recognised, but artefacts of the Abbevillian and Acheulean type had an enormous geographical range, having been found over much of Africa as well as many parts of Europe and Asia.

During the time of Abbevillian men the climate of Europe was so warm that they were able to sleep in the open. They hunted wild animals, but probably depended more on berries, roots and fruit. They roamed through Spain, France and England, never far from the rivers which gave them their necessary water, and preferring always to keep near the deposits of flint and other stone which provided the material for their tools and weapons. In Europe their principal centres were central Spain, south-western France, along the banks of the Seine, Oise, Marne and Somme rivers of northern France, and in southern England. With them lived herds of elephants, soft-nosed rhinoceroses, with horns often a metre in length, sabre-toothed tigers with ferocious fangs, hippopotamuses, bison, wild horses and deer.

Where these men came from is not certain, but as their tools are not found in central or eastern Europe, but only in the west and south-west, it seems probable that they entered Europe from North Africa.

Abbevillian man's characteristic tool was a primitive hand-axe. It was not hafted to a handle and was usually made of flint. It was roughly pear-shaped, pointed at one end and rounded at the other, worked so that he could grasp it firmly. He used it for a number of purposes. The cutting edge, roughly S-shaped, was useful for hacking at a carcase or sawing a piece of wood, and with the pointed end it was possible to grub up roots. It could also be used as a piercing or stabbing instrument.

The flakes struck off during the process of making the hand-axe were also used. With no further trimming, the sharp edges were used as knives and the pointed ends as awls: and by dressing the edges of the flakes they became useful scrapers for cleaning animal skins.

On average, these tools varied in size from ten to twenty centimetres, but a few somewhat longer ones have been found.

No human remains have been found with these tools and it is not possible to tell at what stage of human evolution their makers had reached. The remarkable resemblance in manufacture over such a vast area poses the problem of whether the method was discovered independently in various parts of the world or whether the tool-makers were following a tradition which had spread from a single centre of inspiration. In any case, the continuity of a single style of manufacture throughout hundreds of generations suggests very strongly that they had by this time acquired the power of speech, however simple their communications may have been.

Towards the end of the first interglacial period the increasing cold of the approaching Mindel glaciation seems to have driven the Abbevillians south again, for they were essentially a forest people, and in parts of western and north-western Europe cultural remains make it reasonable to suppose that they were replaced by a new people better able to adapt themselves to the changing environment.

These have been called the Clactonians. They made greater use of flakes, which they produced in large numbers, as hunting weapons, knives and scrapers. This suggests that with the increasing cold and the resultant decline in vegetation, men were becoming more flesh-eating hunters rather than food-gathering vegetarians.

The culture of the Clactonians survived the second advance of the ice, but with the warmer conditions of the second Interglacial newcomers arrived in Europe. They probably came from Africa, using the same route as the Abbevillians, over the landbridge that existed at Gibraltar, but they wandered farther afield than their predecessors.

The skull from Swanscombe and another of the same age from Fontéchevade in the Charente region of south-western France suggest that these new people, the Acheuleans, were nearer present-day man than the earlier inhabitants of France, and their tools were more finely made than those of the Abbe-villians, with some new forms.

This Acheulean culture was spread widely over Africa, Europe and Asia during mid-Pleistocene times, and in Africa it is found in the Nile valley and the Sahara, the Sahara at this time being not yet desert, but a well-watered steppe land supporting vegetation and tropical animals.

From Egypt the Acheulean culture spread to Jordan, Palestine, Syria and Mesopotamia, and then by way of the Persian Gulf to India.

A few Clactonians lingered on after the arrival of the Acheuleans in Europe and there was a blending of industries, but the way of living changed very little as yet.

In Europe there were vast forests of oak and beech, firs, spruce and mountain ash, with willows at the edge of the rivers. Elephants, rhinoceroses, boars and lions roamed through the mid-European forests and in the north were deer, wild goats, brown bears and wolves. Badgers, martens, otters and beavers lived near the waters and over the grasslands browsed wild oxen, bison and wild horses.

Only in the manufacture of flints did Acheulean men advance in culture. They slept and worked mainly in the open, like their predecessors, either on high ground between the river valleys or along the borders of streams and rivers, but a few of their remains have been found in caves or rock shelters.

They were not far removed from the earlier near-humans of Africa, Asia and Europe. They wandered across Europe from Spain and Portugal through France, Germany and Austria, but they did not reach Russia or Poland and the more distant parts of Scandinavia, which were too near the ice. In Great Britain they went as far as Yorkshire and southwards they reached Italy. In France their favourite hunting grounds were in the north, where they found an abundant supply of flint. In central and southern France and in Spain, where flint is scarcer, they used quartzite and quartz, which are more difficult materials to handle, and the implements found here are generally more roughly made.

During this Lower Palaeolithic period more earth movements disturbed the face of Europe. The land of central Germany and France gradually rose and in the Mediterranean it sank. The land-bridges between Italy and North Africa were broken, and the Mediterranean, which until this time had been composed of two vast lakes, became an inland sea, with the narrow channel of the Straits of Messina linking the eastern and western parts.

The Acheuleans in Europe began to improve their implements at an increasing rate. They made hand-axes of flint in a variety of shapes, including pointed ovals and leaf-shapes. They were beginning to understand the way in which stone behaves when it is struck by another stone and the direction in which to strike it in order to break off fragments of the required size and shape. They found that the best material to begin with was a piece of flint which was not too thick and had upper and lower surfaces which were approximately parallel. This shape can often be found naturally, but where such a piece was not readily available they formed it before setting to work on the manufacture of the tool they needed.

They made tools for scraping, dressing skins, for boring holes and for cutting. The flakes they chipped off they turned to good account and made into similar but more delicate instruments. Some were fine enough to use as spearheads and many have been found trimmed into useful knives.

It is not certain whether these tools were still held in the hand or hafted to a wooden handle, but it seems probable that the finer points were attached in some way to a shaft.

For the thousands of years of the second or Great Interglacial period Acheulean man lived in Europe, slowly improving his skill as a stone tool-maker. It was a change of climate which forced him to alter his ways. The third glacial phase was approaching and the weather was becoming drier. The ice sheet which covered Scandinavia began to creep southwards. The mammoth and woolly rhinoceros appeared from the north and the warmth-loving animals migrated southwards.

The mammoth was a specialised form of elephant which had adapted itself to meet the cold. It was no larger than modern elephants but had enormously long, curving tusks. Its skin was more than 2.5 centimetres thick—three times that of a modern elephant—and beneath it had developed a protective layer of fat eight or nine centimetres thick. Its companion, the woolly rhinoceros, was also protected by a coat of fine wool and hair and had two horns, sometimes a metre long, which stuck out just above its snout, one above the other.

With the increasing cold of the Riss glaciation, the Acheuleans were able to adapt themselves. They began to make camps in more sheltered spots under cliffs and even in the entrances of caves. Their flint industry progressed. The daggers and knives, all carefully trimmed, were sharper and their scrapers more efficient.

As the cold grew more intense they used an increasing number of flakes, but now these were struck from the main flint core and more finely finished, in a widespread technique found all over Europe and in many parts of Africa and Asia, which was first recognised in archaeological finds at Levallois, a suburb of Paris.

These Levallois flakes are considered by some archaeologists to be the work of newcomers, but they were probably made by the late Acheuleans. The core of the flint was first trimmed to a shape resembling that of a tortoise by making the under surface flat and the upper surface convex. This in itself was no mean achievement, and was accomplished by striking flakes from the circumference towards the centre. Then the main flakes were struck off, providing tools as efficient as their finer hand-axes of earlier times.

As the ice spread, the flakes were used in the preparation of vast numbers of animal skins, worn as protective clothing against the piercing winds of the increasing cold.

In middle Pleistocene times these Acheulean hand-axe people were living along the river valleys of the Thames and the Somme, as far east as the Irrawaddy valley in Burma, and in Africa along the banks of the Nile, the Vaal river and the Zambezi, as well as the lake shores of east central Africa, where they found an abundance of big game.

We have little idea what these men of early Palaeolithic times looked like. They lived and died mainly in the open, where their bones soon decayed and vanished, or were eaten by wild animals. They probably retained many features of Pithecanthropus—the large teeth, heavy jaws and massive eyebrow ridges, although their brains were developing.

Only when they took to the caves was there a chance of their bones being preserved, and by that time a new race had entered Europe. They, too, took to the shelter of the caves, as the world grew colder, and were the first true cave men.

They left behind them plenty of evidence of their activities and their culture represents the middle part of the Old Stone Age, the Mousterian period.

CHAPTER TWO

The First Cave Men

Where the men of the Middle Palaeolithic Age first came into existence no one yet knows but they arrived in Europe in mid-Pleistocene times, towards the end of the third interglacial period, perhaps from North Africa by the Gibraltar land-bridge, perhaps from the east by way of south-western Asia and central Europe.

Skulls and bones of this man were found and first recognised as a distinct type at Neanderthal, near Düsseldorf in Germany, and he has been named Neanderthal man. The industries which he practised are known as Mousterian, after the rock-shelter of Le Moustier in the Dordogne, where they were found in large quantities.

There were several different races of Neanderthals, and their remains have been found in South Africa, North Africa, Gibraltar, northern and southern Spain, France, the Channel Islands and south-western England, as well as in Palestine, the northern slopes of the Caucasus mountains, the Crimea, the head of the Adriatic, northern Italy, Germany and Belgium. The Neanderthals ranged farther north than their predecessors, and they reached into China.

A tool-making, primitive type of man had been living in Europe since early Pleistocene times, but until the third interglacial period, which began about 180,000 years ago, very few human remains have so far come to light that can be attributed with reasonable certainty to the earlier period.

The Neanderthalers lived in Europe for about a hundred thousand years and were not supplanted until the appearance of our own branch of the human family some fifty to sixty thousand years ago.

Neanderthal man was in some ways similar to the man of Heidelberg, and during the centuries which elapsed between the passing of the Heidelberg race and Neanderthal man's arrival in Europe he may have been evolving in the East, somewhere near where Heidelberg man came into existence, and from there have followed him into Europe.

Wherever he came from, he is important archaeologically, for he belongs to the first people in Europe to leave behind not only relics of their activities, alongside their skeletal remains, but evidence of their thoughts and emotions.

Neanderthal man was a separate species of the same genus as modern man, a form very different from any now living, and it is a difference which far exceeds that which separates the most divergent of living human races.

Some anthropologists consider that he may have been a half-way stage of development of modern man, basing their theory on the fact that some of the Neanderthals found in Palestine show signs of developing certain physical characteristics of modern man, such as a rudimentary chin. For some time after the arrival of modern man the Neanderthals survived and there may have been a certain amount of hybridisation, but further than that there is no evidence to support the suggestion, and they were in all probability a branch which became over-specialised in the course of their physical evolution and did not survive.

The Neanderthal skull was thick and the vault flat, looking as though it had been compressed from the top downwards, especially at the back. He had a receding forehead, large eye orbits, a very wide nasal aperture, huge jowl and no chin, the jaw having a wide ramus and no notch at the top, as in a human jaw. The molars had very short roots compared with human molars and the palate was larger than that of modern man, being very wide in comparison with its length.

The heavy, solid eyebrow ridge, in contrast to the two ridges of modern humans, was similar to that of all the anthropoids except the orang-utans.

This over-development of the face and jaw meant that his neck was so poised that he could not look upwards. The head hung forward, so that he appeared to be crouching all the time, and although he was upright, with thigh bones thinner than

24

those of a gorilla, although thicker than those of modern man, he walked with a shambling, slouching gait. He was not very tall —not much more than 1.5 to 1.6 metres.

The total capacity of the Neanderthal skull was quite high— some 1300 cc compared with the 1450 cc of the average European and 1100 cc to 1300 cc of a modern Australian aborigine. A large brain does not necessarily mean a high intellect, however, for the highest mental processes are controlled by the frontal region of the brain, and with Neanderthal's markedly receding forehead, the frontal region was smaller than that of modern man, his brain being bigger behind and lower in front. His intellectual faculties were differently arranged and the conformation was similar to that of casts of anthropoid skulls.

Mentally and physically he seems to have been on a different level from modern humans, and it is not certain whether he could speak, although he was probably able to make some rudimentary form of spoken communication. He may have been covered with hair, which would support the theory that he was a species of sub-human which had adapted itself to living in arctic conditions and faded out of existence when a warmer climate prevailed.

Shortly after his arrival in Europe the rigours of the fourth phase of the Ice Age approached. The ice fields from Scandinavia and the Alps once more spread slowly down the mountains and over the plains of central Europe. To the south, where the ice did not reach, the climate was as bleak as Labrador, and only as far south as North Africa was it temperate.

The mammoth and the woolly rhinoceros, great oxen and reindeer slowly migrated southwards from the tundra of Russia to the cold steppes of central and southern Europe, but in the sheltered parts of the continent, particularly the south of France, a few warmth-loving animals lingered on, despite the increasing cold.

The fourth glacial epoch, though not so cold as the second or third, was nevertheless severe. The ice fields from Scandinavia did not reach Great Britain this time, but Britain was covered in the north by glaciers which flowed from the Scottish highlands to the sea. Much of England was as cold as the arctic regions and in the valley of the Thames (which was then still a tributary of the Rhine) there roamed reindeer, woolly rhinoceroses and mammoths.

The Mousterian period of Neanderthal man can be divided into three stages. First was the cool, dry period, the time when the Acheuleans were still practising their hand-axe industry and the hippopotamuses, rhinoceroses and elephants still lingered in northern and southern France, when herds of bison, cattle and wild horses roamed through Europe and men still lived in the open, seeking only occasionally the shelter of the cliffs and rock grottoes.

With the approach of the ice, the second part of the Mousterian period began. The Acheulean industry faded, merging with the Mousterian, and Acheulean man disappears from the scene. Animals and birds from the arctic regions entered Europe and the Neanderthalers moved to the entrances of caves and grottoes for shelter.

The final stage came during the peak of the fourth glaciation, when arctic animals spread over Europe and Mousterian man sought permanent shelter in the caves, except during his summer hunting expeditions.

At first his implements were similar to those of the Acheuleans and difficult to distinguish from them, although the method of manufacture was individual. They included chipped stone-axes and tools for scraping and chopping, mostly made from flakes by the Levallois method, in which the flint was specially prepared before the flake was struck from it.

This flake industry was characteristic of the Mousterian period during the height of Neanderthal man's activity in Europe. Throughout France and England Mousterian workshops have been found on the flint beds, with numbers of half-finished implements scattered around, as well as fragments of flaked and finished tools. From these littered remains it has been possible to reconstruct his method of working. The piece of flint was first knocked into a roughly suitable size and shape. Then the flakes were removed from the flint surface. With one blow, he was able to strike off a single large flake, which had one smooth surface where it had broken from the main core, the other having been carefully fashioned from the preliminary flaking. The result was a neat, sharp-edged implement which was again carefully trimmed. In this way, tools for piercing, cutting, scraping and sawing were made, many of them reaching a high standard of workmanship well in advance of the Acheulean culture.

Spearheads have been found with notched bases, indicating

26

that they had been fastened, possibly with animal sinew, to shafts which were probably of wood, to make more effective hunting weapons. Balls of limestone have also been found, varying in size from about four centimetres to ten centimetres, which could have been used, with strips of leather or sinew, as sling stones for killing game.

Though he was forced to spend months at a time sheltering in caves, he was still primarily a hunter, for he subsisted on wild animals. He may have been mainly vegetarian in the first place and taken to eating meat when the cold increased and vegetation became scarcer. His weapons were small and could not have been particularly effective in open conflict with the beasts he sought to kill, some of which were as large or larger than himself, so he may have used game-traps—deep pits with sharp-pointed spikes implanted round the sides at an angle, so that when the animal fell into one, it was impaled and helpless.

The hafted spears would have been useful when the animal was at the water or making a river crossing, but it is more than likely that the Mousterians did not attempt to kill these animals single-handed but hunted in groups. They had no social organisation yet, but the family of parents and children, which is a biological grouping, was established as a unit and families may well have lived together for mutual protection, in groups of about twenty or thirty, the able-bodied men engaging in hunting expeditions and bringing in stores of game and meat, fat, skins and bones, as well as lumps of raw flint on which to work, while the women remained in the camp, looking after their children and caring for the old and infirm, who were respected for the cultural traditions and useful hunting lore they were able to pass on to the younger generations.

Their prey was bison, wild cattle, horses, reindeer, rhinoceroses, giant deer and cave bears, with bison and cave bears predominating. They used fire, but whether they cooked their food it is impossible to say. They cut up the game where it died and took away the best joints and the large bones, cracked open the skull for the brains and ripped off the skin. When they had eaten the flesh from the bones, they split them open for the marrow and threw them on the fire.

Some Mousterian remains consist entirely of these broken bones. Many were no doubt used as tools, with little or no further trimming, but some have scratch marks, suggesting that they may have been used as anvils for shaping their finer flint tools.

An examination of their remains shows that they suffered from various ills. The member of the race found at Neanderthal had suffered a fracture of the inner bone of the forearm. The bone of the left upper arm had also been injured at some time, which no doubt made it a good deal weaker than the right arm. And although there is no real evidence of malnutrition, the condition of the bones has suggested that he may have been suffering from rickets.

A man found at La Chapelle-aux-Saints had lost many of his teeth before death, which may have been due to pyorrhoea or decay, but the only two teeth still in his jaw were sound. In the jaw of a woman found at Ehringsdorf all the teeth are intact except two, but she was suffering from pyorrhoea and had an abscess in the region of the left canine.

Of the five hundred fragments of Neanderthaloid bones examined in a find at Krapina in Yugoslavia many showed signs of arthritis, particularly some vertebrae and a kneecap, and one of the group had broken his collar bone, but it had healed well before his death.

At La Quina a man died whose teeth were sound except for tartar deposits and traces of gingivitis.

These men and women, sub-human though they were, suffered from ills which we all know and understand, and they also had emotions over and above those connected with the physical needs of warmth, shelter and sex—the emotions which arose from the basic desire of all mankind to survive, either in this world or the next.

During the winter there were periods when, for weeks at a time, they could not stir from their caves. There is no evidence that they invented lamps, but day after day they sat round their fires, chipping their flint implements, preparing their food, cleaning and scraping the skins for warm clothing, passing the time till the next hunting season.

Being thrown together in this way, they grew to know one another better. Their powers of communication, even if it were not yet fully articulated speech, must have improved. They had time to think, to exchange ideas, to feel affection for one another.

Sometimes, when a member of the group died, the body was no longer disregarded and left to its fate amongst the wild animals. They buried it with careful ritual in the cave where they lived, sometimes near the hearth, possibly in the hope that the warmth of the fire would give it life again. The burial was usually in the pre-natal, crouched, sleeping position, often with the head to the west, towards the setting sun; and with the body they placed food and some of their finest implements, presumably for the journey to the next world.

Already these pre-humans seem to have been aware of an external power, higher than any skills or devices which they could command of their own volition—a mysterious force which ultimately governed their existence. They were perhaps experiencing religious emotions which began with this early human consciousness and were to be one of the most potent forces affecting man's future history. In this first intellectual struggle with the mystery of death Neanderthal man grappled in a variety of ways, unwilling to accept the conception of total extinction.

In a cave at Le Moustier, in the Dordogne region of France, were found the buried remains of a Neanderthal youth of about sixteen years of age. His head lay on a small pile of carefully arranged stones. Close to his right hand, ready for his use, was a beautifully worked hand-axe, and near by were the remains of meat which had been buried with him.

Under a low cliff in the same district, at La Ferrassie, were found several graves of Neanderthal children, in some of which tools had been placed. One grave was covered with a large stone bearing a dozen small, artificially-cut pittings arranged in pairs, the meaning of which is obscure, though they could have been some sort of record, and similar cup-markings have been found in the work of much later people. Not far away, in the Corréze region, at the little village of La Chapelle-aux-Saints, the grave of an old man was found, who had been buried with equal care, surrounded by offerings of food, flint and quartz implements.

In some Alpine caves have been found skulls and bones, mainly of cave bears, arranged with precision and strongly suggesting that they were shrines for propitiating the spirit of the cave bear, either as a protection against it or to ensure a good hunt, an indication that man was moving towards a desire to gain power over unseen and uncomprehended forces of nature by magic.

Something happened to the Neanderthals to put an end to the Mousterian culture. Perhaps they were defeated in the end by the cold and the increasing difficulties of securing food. A new and finer race of men appeared in Europe towards the end of the fourth glaciation and the Neanderthals slowly disappeared, although a later race of men living in eastern Europe during the later years of the Old Stone Age possessed certain Neanderthal physical characteristics.

Apart from these people, who practised the Solutrean culture, there is no evidence that the Neanderthal races existed later than forty or fifty thousand years ago. They and the Mousterian culture died out and with them ended the middle period of the Old Stone Age.

CHAPTER THREE

The End of the Ice Age

While the Neanderthals were living through the last stages of
their existence, during the fourth glacial epoch, new races of
men were coming into existence. Modern man had at last
appeared on the scene, at the stage of evolution from his anthropoid forbears which we all represent today. He was still a
hunting savage, but he possessed remarkable technical skills,
outstanding artistic gifts and religious emotions more clearly
defined than those of Neanderthal man, although at first they
were expressed in terms of simple magic.

The earliest discovery of this new race of men was made more
than a hundred years ago, in the cave of Paviland, amongst the
limestone cliffs of the South Wales coast. First the remains of
mammoths, rhinoceroses, bears, horses, reindeer and hyenas
came to light and then the young man himself. Before burial his
body had been painted with red ochre, symbolic of the life-
giving blood he had lost at death, and which was thereby
'restored' to him, in the hope that it would give him new life.
It was one of the earliest examples of sympathetic magic and
one of the longest-lasting practices, for the custom of sprink-
ling the dead body with red ochre continued for another twenty
thousand years.

At Les Eyzies in the Dordogne region of France a number of
similar humans were discovered, near the overhanging rocks of
Cro-Magnon, after which this people and their various racial
modifications have been named. One of them had received a sharp
blow on the forehead, from which he recovered before he died,
and at least one old man was suffering badly from pyorrhoea.

31

At the grotto of Aurignac, on the French side of the Pyrenees, a large Cro-Magnon cemetery was discovered, containing more human remains of this race and implements of a distinctive culture, which henceforth was called Aurignacian.

Remains of Cro-Magnon men have since been found, much about the same age in archaeological history, throughout Europe, North and West Africa, the Middle East and Asia, already possessing physical characteristics of the modern races of the world, and it seems probable that they originated in western Asia and migrated to Europe, some by way of the plains of eastern Turkestan and southern Russia and others through the valleys of the Tigris and Euphrates rivers, Syria, Palestine, North Africa and Spain.

How they came to reach a stage of development so far in advance of the Neanderthals is still a mystery. One theory is that they evolved from a group of anthropoids who left their forest home for the plains, far back in Tertiary times, a million or more years ago, at a time when the forests were dwindling in extent. Finding themselves ill-equipped for competing with other land animals for food, they made their way to the tropical sea-shores and developed a taste for sea-food. For many years they lived by the water's edge, taking their food from the rock pools and shallows, and then, gradually becoming more venturesome, waded out to the deeper waters and acquired the ability to swim.

Spending increasing lengths of time in the water, it is thought that they eventually lost their hairy coats, though, as their heads remained above water as they swam, they kept their head hair, which was a useful protection from the sun.

During these years they were making simple tools for cracking open the shells of the crustaceans, which were their most important source of food, and when their tool-making had reached the necessary state of proficiency, they moved away from the sea-shores and tested their fortunes as land-hunters.

There is no firm evidence yet for this theory nor does it help with the missing evidence of the stages by which he became a modern man, though there is something to be said for the idea that he could have evolved from a Neanderthaloid race which developed in Asia, in a different way from the European Neanderthals.

The Cro-Magnons may have first reached Europe some fifty thousand years ago. By 30,000 B.C. they were well established, particularly in south-western France and northern Spain, and the cultures by which they are represented are known collectively as the upper part of the Old Stone Age or the Upper Palaeolithic.

During the first advance of the fourth period of the ice age, the Würm glaciation, the Neanderthals were still the only men in Europe, living in their rock shelters. At the climax of this glaciation, ice sheets from the Scottish highlands and the mountains of Scandinavia covered most of Britain north of the Thames, and the north German plain as far as Berlin. Glaciers radiated from the Alps and the Pyrenees, and on the bleak tundras bordering the ice and on the cold steppes roamed herds of mammoths, woolly rhinoceroses, bison, wild horses and reindeer.

The Würm glaciation was interrupted by a warm phase, after which conditions became almost glacial again before rising slowly to the temperatures which prevail today: and it was during this warm interlude that the Cro-magnons arrived, ready armed with efficient tools for hunting the game which they found in abundance.

They were tall, varying in height between 1.7 metres and 2 metres, with well-developed features, including high foreheads and firm chins. The skulls are indistinguishable from those of contemporary human beings and their brain capacity was somewhat larger than that of the average modern man. Moreover, a development of the tongue muscles made it possible for them to speak with ease and communicate their thoughts.

The evolution of the brain of Cro-Magnon man had conferred on him the quality of humanity, for it had developed the capacity for learning from experience, at the expense of the instinctive tendencies of other living creatures. This had come about through the development of special powers of sight, touch and hearing. He had a unique power of vision and a capacity to understand what he saw in terms of form, colour and texture, as well as an ability to recognise his fellow human beings and interpret their expressions.

This visual discrimination was accompanied by an increase in muscular skill and control, which enabled him to attain a fully upright position, and this in its turn gave him a wider visual range. The evolution of vision also gave him a more delicate sense of touch and the hands became infinitely more skilful.

Mankind thus acquired a store of experience and knowledge, some from his own life, some communicated to him by his fellow human beings: and ever since these first days of his existence, the activities of all human beings have involved the principle of continuity from past experience, made possible by the brain's infinite capacity for recording them.

He is thus able to use his brain during all the processes of living and has become an individual. This has imposed on him the need to build up for himself modes of conduct which do not conform to any general laws of nature. Paradoxically, however, these mental powers which have given him the opportunity to extend his range of knowledge have also provided him with conventions and traditions which have channelled his thoughts along well-worn conventions and made him, generally speaking, obstinately averse from changing the patterns of life and thought his intellect has created. He has become a prisoner within the confines of his own traditions, unreceptive to new thinking and ways of life. The cultures leading up to the first true civilisation developed very slowly, mainly by learning and copying from each other; and the big strides were made by the few men of genius, born into nearly every generation, who alone seem able to escape from the inertia of tradition.

Cro-Magnon man was living in Europe from 35,000 to 10,000 B.C. Five main cultures of this Upper Palaeolithic period are distinguishable but this does not represent five stages in development at five separate levels. In places one or more of the stages are absent, for it was a time of migrations and inter-mingling of the races.

The radio-carbon dating of the cultures gives 32,000 to 28,500 B.C. for the earliest—the Chatelperronian—which was confined to south-western France. Next came the Aurignacian, which was wide-ranging and dates from 28,500 B.C. to 22,000 B.C. The Gravettian occurs in the northerly parts of Europe and finds are dated from 22,000 B.C. to 18,000 B.C. The intrusive Solutrean culture, short-lived in Europe, was from 18,000 B.C. to 15,000 B.C., and the final phase, the Magdalenian, was from 15,000 B.C. to 8000 B.C.

At the beginning of this Upper Palaeolithic period the shapes of the continents had assumed much of their present form, except that the Mediterranean was still two lakes with land-bridges at Sicily and Gibraltar, and the North Sea and the English Channel were still largely dry land, with the Thames meeting the Rhine somewhere east of the Straits of Dover.

The Cro-Magnons who practised the Chatelperronian culture of south-eastern France were indistinguishable in physical appearance from the people living there today. A large proportion of their flint tools were very similar to those of Mousterian times and it is sometimes difficult to tell them apart. They may, in fact, have settled in the entrances of the rock shelters and caves where the last of the Neanderthals still lingered. Legends of ogres and monstrous human beings may even have been derived from the folk memory of the Cro-Magnons who first encountered the last of these strange near-humans, who now vanish from the scene, though there is no evidence that they suffered any violent end.

The Cro-Magnons who succeeded the Chatelperronians, the Aurignacians, achieved a clear advance in techniques. Their culture is widespread, industries of the Aurignacian type having been found as far east as northern Iraq and Afghanistan, in Syria and Palestine and, moving westwards, in Transcaucasia and the Crimea, Rumania, Hungary, Austria, southern Germany, France and Spain.

Britain was still too cold and remote to attract the Aurignacians in any great numbers. Perhaps a few hundred reached this corner of Europe. Caves in Derbyshire, north and south Wales, the Wye valley and the Mendips were occupied for short spells, but the tools they left behind were few and of poor quality.

As Europe grew warmer, the Cro-Magnons emerged from their caverns and began to explore the plains and valleys. They were magnificent hunters and also fishermen. They made a great variety of stone and flint scrapers, including end-scrapers, in which the blade was worked at one end only, and side-scrapers, in which the whole of one side was trimmed to form a working edge. Small flint points had very sharp, knife-like blades and with the passing years they devised an increasing variety of new tools, as well as more efficient types of the old-established forms. The end-scrapers grew more efficient, the side-scrapers were made with an inward curving edge to trim curved surfaces, the awls and knives were sharper.

The characteristic tool of the Aurignacians was the engraving burin, which was very similar in form to the burin used today

35

by engravers on metal. This they used for working antler and bone and also for decorative engraving on their tools and weapons.

Towards the end of Aurignacian times in Europe, the Cro-Magnons did their finest work in bone or ivory, rather than flint, making beautiful spearheads and a variety of boring implements. Fine bone points have been found, notched at one end, and although they have not been pierced they may well have been the first needles, for they could have carried a thread of sinew through hide or fur. They had certainly begun to take an interest in their appearance, for they made bone and ivory bracelets as well as beads, which were strung together on sinew for necklaces.

Before the onset of the next period of cold it was a time of plenty in Europe. With a generous and readily accessible food supply, the population increased and they had time on their hands. They began to experiment in drawing and painting and in western Europe the earliest results of their attempts to portray the animals of their world can be seen on the walls of caves and rock shelters, mostly engraved in outline with their burins. These skills were to develop into the wonderful cave art of their descendants, the Magdalenians.

The first need of all living creatures is for food and the drawing of these animals was, most likely, not primarily an artistic urge but a manifestation of man's desire to achieve, by magical means, their continued abundance and his ability to secure them.

With the return of the cold during the last phase of the Würm glaciation the woodlands of western Europe once more dwindled and gave way to steppes and tundra. A new culture emerged, adapted to the new conditions. This was the Gravettian, which is found in western and central Europe, including Great Britain, where Gravettian remains have been found at Cresswell Crags in Derbyshire, and as far east as the Ukraine and southern Russia.

The Gravettians hunted the mammoth, bison and wild horse over the cold steppes, and their arrows and spearheads were tipped with flint, in contrast to the bone tips of the Aurignacians. Living on the wind-swept, open plains, their only hope of survival was to build protective huts. These were simple shelters dug half a metre or so into the ground, surmounted by a framework of saplings and boughs, made wind-proof with heaped-up earth, and roofed with hides.

In the loess lands of Russia, where many Gravettian remains have come to light, their huts have been found built in close groups, presumably with a family to a hut, the huts varying in size from about four metres to seven metres in diameter. As their principal prey was the huge mammoth, it seems more than likely that they hunted in fairly large groups, for the mammoth would have been more than a match for a single hunter.

The characteristic art form of the Gravettians was the carved ivory or soft-stone female figurine, usually depicted as pregnant. The figures are highly stylised and the facial features are seldom even indicated. The discoveries of these little female figures are widespread, having turned up in southern and south-western France, north Italy and throughout central Europe as far as the south Russian plain.

Often the head is represented by a mere nob, the arms are insignificant and the legs taper away from the thighs into form-lessness, the whole emphasis being on the breasts and buttocks. Two have been found which were decorated with red ochre.

These 'Venus' figures are another aspect of man's principal preoccupation—his search for the means of preserving his own life and surviving. Not yet correlating cause and effect, he seems to have believed that an effigy of a life-giving woman combined with a substance which was the colour of blood would preserve the life of the living and restore it to those who had lost it by death. The effigy and the red ochre were 'Givers of Life' and the search for similar elixirs to safeguard man's existence were the inspiration of primitive religion.

Of the Venus of Brassempuy in south-western France only the head survives, but it is beautifully carved from mammoth ivory and was probably painted, although hardly any traces of colour have survived. It is only between 2.5 and 3 cm long, but the hair is indicated and also the eyes and nose. The limestone Venus of Willendorf is larger, the whole body being preserved, but in this example the head is stylised and the hair and face are not indicated at all. At Laussel, Venus figures carved in low relief on limestone blocks have been found, the most striking being that of a pregnant women with full breasts and swelling thighs, holding up a bison horn in her right hand. The figure is full face and was probably painted originally with red ochre, but the ochre has worn away and the facial features have disappeared.

The Gravettians also carved animals, and in Czechoslovakia animal figures in fire-hardened clay have been found. Like the Aurignacians, they engraved them on the walls of caves and also on stone slabs, pieces of bone and pebbles. In Cantabria a broken fragment of stone was found on which the figure of a horse had been engraved. Only the hindquarters and two back legs have survived, but they are magnificently vigorous and realistic, suggesting that once these people had acquired the skill to portray animal and human figures for their magical and religious rites, they had begun to take an artistic delight in their creation.

At Colombière a number of pebbles of the same age as the Cantabrian horse came to light, engraved with all manner of animals—reindeer, musk ox, rhinoceroses, cave bears and chamois.

Engraving seems to have been rarer in eastern and central Europe and there was no cave art, but personal ornaments as well as numerous bone and ivory tools have been discovered, all of them ornamented with engraved, simple linear patterns.

On the walls of Cro-Magnon caves in France imprints of hands have been found, some of which give the impression that fingers or the joints of fingers were missing. This may have been because of imperfect impressions, but finger mutilation has been widespread amongst primitive people until comparatively recent times.

W. J. Burchell, writing in 1824 of his travels in South Africa, said: "I met an old woman ... who stopped to show me her hands, and made me observe that the little finger of the right hand had lost two joints and that of the left, one. She explained ... that they had been cut off at different times to express grief ... for the death of three daughters. After this I looked more attentively at those I met and saw many other women, and some of the men with their bones mutilated in the same manner; but it was only the little fingers which were thus shortened."

Another explanation of the Bushmen's self-mutilation was that they wanted to ensure a safe journey to the next world and a life of ease and plenty when they arrived. Elsewhere in Africa the practice was a therapy for certain illnesses. The Indians of north-west Canada sacrificed a little finger at a funeral, in the hope that death would not visit their tribe again for many months. Captain Cook observed the practice in the Tonga Islands, where it was done to win the favour of their most important god, and the custom was common throughout the Pacific.

Usually, the more widespread a custom of this kind, the older its origins; so it may well be that finger mutilation spread from the Cro-Magnons who practised it during some magical rite of their own devising.

Some of the Cro-Magnon burials were full length, but more were in the pre-natal, crouched position and the dead person was always provided with gifts of food and weapons and life-giving red ochre.

In the cave of Grimaldi near Mentone, two skeletons were found, side by side. They were a youth of fifteen or sixteen and a middle-aged woman who was probably his mother. They lay in a shallow grave, in a crouching position, and their bodies had been ornamented with shell bracelets and bead ornaments.

The cave had been previously inhabited by Mousterians, for there were Mousterian implements and bones of the straight-tusked elephant and rhinoceros scattered about in the layer of débris in which they rested.

At first they were thought to have been Negroes, but certain features of the skull, noticeably the shape of the forehead, dis-proved this, being more typically Cro-Magnon. Yet the long forearm, curved thigh bone and heavy jaw were more anthro-poidal than either Neanderthal or Cro-Magnon man. The Grimaldis may have represented an intermediate stage between Negroes as we know them today and the Cro-Magnons, for at this time the Negroes were already on the move in Africa, some coming into Spain and France over the Gibraltar land-bridge.

Whoever the Grimaldis were and wherever they came from, they seem to have met with little success, and do not appear again in Europe.

At Solutré in central France the skeleton of a tall man was found with a skull which was rounder than that of the older-established, long-headed Cro-Magnons, and he is thought to have been an early member of the Alpine people who today live throughout northern and central Europe and in parts of central Asia. At Combe Capelle in the Dordogne and at Engis in Belgium human remains in Aurignacian levels can be identified with the long-headed Mediterranean people of Spain, Italy, North Africa, Egypt, Arabia, Iran, India and Pakistan, and another skull from Combe Capelle seems to have had an affinity with the Nordic people of Scandinavia.

Thus by the end of Aurignacian and Gravettian times, some twenty thousand years ago, there were four or five distinct types in Europe, the Cro-Magnons, the Grimaldis, the Alpines, the Mediterraneans and perhaps the Nordics, but for many years to come the Cro-Magnons were dominant and the problem of how and where the various races of the world began to diverge is still unsolved. The divergencies seem to have arisen through a slow genetic differentiation following the widespread migrations and colonisation of uninhabited territories which took place at the end of the Ice Age. Until this time men had occupied only the warmer part of the Old World, Africa, Europe, western Asia, India, south-eastern Asia and Indonesia. But as the ice retreated large tracts of new land became available, and as they were occupied the settlers in the more remote parts of the world tended to become isolated.

Pigmentation was an adaptation to climate and so, in all probability, was the epicanthic fold of the Mongolian eye and the width of the nasal aperture, which became extremely narrow among the Eskimos and wide amongst the Africans.

During the cold period in which the Gravettians were active another Upper Palaeolithic people arrived in Europe for a relatively short spell. From their work found at Solutré they are known as the Solutreans and they seem to have come from the east, through Hungary, where many deposits of their remains have been found, and along the Danube valley. They introduced a new method of flaking flints which nevertheless had some affinity with that of the Mousterians, and they may have been distant relations of a branch of the Neanderthals which lingered on in eastern Europe or descendants of an ancestral branch of the Cro-Magnons, with whom they compare in stature. The skeleton of a Solutrean found at Brünn, in Czechoslovakia, shows a tall man with a powerful neck and shoulders, a long head and strong chin, and close by were the scattered remains of woolly rhinoceroses and mammoths, as well as perforated shell beads, stone discs, bone ornaments made from the teeth and ribs of mammoths, and an ivory figurine.

At Předmost, fifty miles to the east, a cache of more than twenty thousand Solutrean implements was found, as well as numbers of hearths and the remains of men, women and children, with their bone and stone tools, their ivory beads and small figurines.

They were hunters and spread over much of western Europe. They do not seem to have reached Britain, though influences of their distinctive method of tool-making have been found as far north as Derbyshire and as far west as Paviland. Nor did they reach the Mediterranean, but they spread through central France and Spain, where they came into contact with Africans, from whom they learnt the use of the bow and arrow.

In parts of central Europe the Solutreans seem to have been more powerful than the Cro-Magnons for a time, usurping their hunting grounds, but the Cro-Magnons survived and continued their way of life.

The Solutreans were cave dwellers during the winter months but they camped in the open when the weather was milder, preferring the open plains and hardly ever reaching even the lower hills.

A number concentrated in the Charente and Dordogne regions of France. They were not artists or painters but supremely skilled in stone working, making delicately fashioned lanceheads and arrowheads, flaking the stone by pressure and achieving a wonderful symmetry. At the height of their achievements two main, characteristic weapons emerged, both of them leaf-shaped. One was broad like a laurel leaf, the other narrow as a willow leaf, and they varied in size from small arrowheads no more than two or three centimetres long, used for spearing fish or small game, to spearheads which were up to thirty centimetres in length.

In late Solutrean times, newer forms appeared. The arrowheads and darts had stems, for easier hafting to shafts, and also houlders or tangs at the base, which made the first barbed weapons. They also seem to have made the first, slender little bone sewing needles, which were pierced with an eye.

Towards the end of their time in Europe, about 16,000 to 15,000 B.C., their work declined in quality. The second cold spell of the last glaciation was approaching, and rather than adapt themselves they moved to warmer latitudes. At the same time a new generation of Cro-Magnons came to predominance in Europe, their way of life admirably suited to the approaching glacial conditions. These were the Magdalenians, named after La Madeleine, near Les Eyzies, in the Dordogne, where so many of their remains have come to light.

Europe was cold and damp, and after a brief spell of warmer weather, conditions became glacial again as, with the second phase of the fourth glaciation, the ice began to spread over Europe, and the continent became once more the home of the reindeer, stag, deer, bison, horse, ass, musk ox, antelope and arctic hare, though the mammoth had by now become extinct. There were fewer horses than in Solutrean times, but many more reindeer.

The Magdalenians spread over a relatively limited area of Europe, ranging from west and south-west Germany through to France and the Cantabrian region of Spain. A few examples of their bone-work have been found in Great Britain, at Kent's Cavern near Torquay and in the West Riding of Yorkshire, but no human remains have come to light. They were hunters, forced by the climate to spend long spells in rock shelters and caves, although in milder periods they lived in tents or sunken huts. Their standard of living seems to have been no great advance on that of their Aurignacian ancestors, but their culture, unaffected by the intrusive Solutreans, was enriched by a wider range of skills and above all by the development of their inherited artistic gifts, which culminated in their outstanding achievements in painting and sculpture, both of which were apparently developed from their magico-religious beliefs.

Their material culture is characterised by the use of bone and reindeer antler, which was available in abundance and from which they made a wide range of weapons and implements as well as personal ornaments.

They made plain and barbed points of antler and bone, which were attached with sinews to wooden shafts, the barbs sometimes on only one side of the point, sometimes on both. Two or three points were sometimes mounted together to make a fishing spear, similar to those used until the present century by Fijians. They used the bow and arrow and the spear thrower, an ingenious mechanical device for lengthening the throw of a spear, little different from that used by Australian aborigines, Eskimos and many primitive tribes of South America. They made shaft straighteners, fish hooks and whistles; and all these artefacts were decorated with delicate engravings of animals of the chase.

The Magdalenians carved bone needles with which to sew their reindeer skin clothing. They had stone lamps, similar in shape to those of present-day Eskimos, which they used for both light and heat, burning animal oil with wicks of moss. And they devised all manner of personal ornaments, necklaces of bear, horse and reindeer teeth, land and sea shells, as well as pendants and hairpins of bone and ivory.

The arts of engraving, sculpture and painting, begun in Aurignacian times, revived and developed. In the dim recesses of the caves of the Dordogne of south-west central France, the French and Spanish Pyrenees and the Cantabrian mountains of northern Spain, away from the damaging effects of sun, rain and wind, their work has been marvellously preserved, and the naked footprints of the artists, their palettes, and fragments of the paint they used for their work were found when the caves were rediscovered and explored some ten thousand years later.

At first the Magdalenian artists drew in outline with fine, flint points. Innumerable engravings on mammoth ivory, bone and antler, on pebbles and even on lumps of amber and ochre, have been found, as well as the animal engravings on the cave walls. Then they experimented with sculpture, modelling animals and human figures in stone, bone and clay. Later still they began to paint, very often making an engraved outline drawing first. Their colours were mainly black, red, brown and yellow, and lumps of red and brown ochre and oxide of manganese have been found in the caves, along with the horns in which they stored them, stone pestles and mortars for grinding them and stone palettes. If a suitably curving surface of rock presented itself, they would use it for the body of the animal, to give a three-dimensional realism.

At the cavern of Combarelles, in the Dordogne, there are nearly four hundred Magdalenian drawings of horses, rhinoceroses, mammoths, reindeer, bison, stags, ibex, lions and wolves, and at the famous cave of Altamira, in northern Spain, is some of the finest work of the Old Stone Age yet discovered—incised drawings, outline drawings in black, and paintings in red, brown, black and yellow, of bison, horses, red deer and wild boars, some drawn singly, others in groups, but all of them naturalistic, carefully observed and full of an amazing vitality. Each picture seems to be a living portrait of an animal which the artist knew.

They could be interpreted as a manifestation of the primitive hunter's recognition of his dependence on the animals for his existence—an emotion which, judging from the supreme artistry of the work, was so deeply felt that it may be called a religious experience although at this stage it was probably little more than a vague awareness of the existence of a supernatural power of limitless range, far above and beyond man's control, which was to be felt in every aspect of nature, animals and trees, rivers and rocks, and the abstract forces of sun and wind, thunder and storm. This was a pre-animistic religion, for true animism imbues all these elements with separate and personal spirits.

To the Magdalenian, the animals of his daily life were possessed of this cosmic spirit. He regarded them as stronger than himself, both physically and spiritually, and since he had to kill some of them in order to live, he sought to secure their blessing first.

Examples of this way of thinking were recorded late in the last century by observers among the hunting tribes of Lapland, Siberia, north-east Asia and North America. Among the Tlingit Indians of Alaska, for example, when a bear was brought into camp "its head was carried indoors and eagle down and red paint put upon it. Then one talked to it as if to a human being, saying, 'I am your friend, I am poor and come to you.' Before the entrails were burned he talked to it saying, 'I am poor, that is why I am hunting you.' When one came to a bear trail, he said, 'My father's brother-in-law, have pity upon me, let me be in luck.' "*

Among the Koryaks of north-east Siberia, when a bear is killed, "the bear-skin is taken off along with the head and one of the women puts on the skin, dances in it, and entreats the bear not to be angry, but to be kind to the people".†

Although the Magdalenians may have painted near the mouths of the caves, and the paintings weathered away throughout the centuries, the very fact that they seem to have chosen the darkest and most remote corners of the caves for their work is significant, for another observer has recorded that before a hunt Apache medicine men "used to resort to certain caves where they pro-

* Swanton, *The Tlingit Indians*, p. 455.
† Jochelson, *The Koryak*, p. 88.

pitiated the animal gods whose progeny they intended to
destroy".*

It would seem, therefore, that the Magdalenians, having
acquired the ability to reproduce the animals, which they needed
to hunt for their subsistence, felt that the image gave them power
over them and would make the hunt simpler and safer.

Some they painted with a large heart in the middle, pierced by
an arrow, an example of sympathetic magic similar to the nail
fetishes of West Africa and the Congo, and the little male dolls
which have turned up in quite recent times in country districts
of Britain, pierced by a pin, as a token of vengeance, by the
distracted girl who had been jilted.

The Magdalenian artists needed their lamps as they worked,
and even so it is difficult to see sometimes how they reached the
spots where the paintings were made, unless they stood on each
other's shoulders.

The grotto of Pasiega near Castillo, in the Santander province
of northern Spain, is a strange, winding cavern, the walls of
which are covered with animal paintings, and at the far end is a
limestone cavern, which seems to have been a primitive chapel
where Magdalenian men observed their magical rites.

Some of the paintings are extraordinarily like the Bushman
rock shelter paintings of Rhodesia, and centuries after the Bushmen had been driven from Rhodesia into the deserts of the Kala-
hari and south-west Africa, the Bantu-speaking Negroes who
replaced them regarded these spots as sacred. In a rock shelter
a few miles from Salisbury are found animal paintings of horses
and stylised human beings, with dashes representing water, which
suggest that the rain god was involved. At another spot drawings
of kudu (African antelopes), rhinoceroses and human figurines
with elongated arms and legs occur, one of the human beings
pouring water over a tree. This became a Bantu place of pil-
grimage in time of drought, the pilgrims bringing placatory
offerings to the rain god and thereby continuing the tradition
established by the earlier Bushmen.

The Magdalenians seldom represented the human figure and
when they did it was not naturalistic but a grotesque, sometimes
wearing an animal mask, the most famous being in the cave of
Trois Frères, in the lower slopes of the Pyrenees, not far from

* N. W. Thomas, *Animals in Hastings*, E.R.I., i, 511b.

St. Girons. The entrance passage is narrow and difficult, but it divides into three branches, and the left-hand branch dips steeply, ending in an alcove, the walls of which are covered with engravings of bison, horses, lions, mammoths, reindeer, rhinocerouses and cave bears. In the far wall is a natural tunnel at ground level, again decorated with animal engravings on its walls and ceiling, which takes a right-handed bend and then slopes steeply upwards, to end in an aperture some four metres above the alcove.

To the right of the aperture, looking down on to the alcove, is the figure, partly painted, partly engraved, of a man wearing a stag's mask with antlers. This seems to be a development from the conception of the animal guardian spirit to the more sophisticated idea of the totem animal, the totem being a man's especial animal guardian, revealed to him in a dream or inherited from his father, in which case it becomes a family totem. Alternatively, the totem animal may be the common guardian of the whole tribe of hunters.

Ceremonial animal masks were common enough amongst primitive peoples, worn during their tribal rituals, as part of their equipment for imitating the totem and assimilating his more desirable characteristics of courage and strength. Human forms wearing animal masks are to be seen in Egyptian murals and on Babylonian seals: and in the present century they were used in many parts of West Africa and the Congo, amongst the Indians of the north-west coast of America, throughout many of the islands of the Pacific and in Tibet, during the mystery plays of the Lama ceremonies—strange rituals which seem to have persisted since the Stone Age.

Towards the end of Magdalenian times, the precision in animal drawing was not so marked and the representations became conventionalised, perhaps because the magical significance having become so well established, the detail was no longer necessary for the purpose it was intended to serve.

The climate was changing. It was becoming warmer. The glaciers retreated to the high mountains and the Scandinavian and Scottish ice sheets melted and shrank. In what is now temperate Europe, forests replaced the steppe and tundra. The environment of the Magdalenians changed and hunting became more difficult. With increasing warmth, the reindeer moved northwards and eastwards, followed by the bison and the horse, and they lost an important source of food and clothing, as well as bone and horn for their manufactures.

Some of the Magdalenians may have followed the reindeer north-eastwards across Europe and Asia, for it was during these late glacial times that Siberia was first populated, nd settlements of people have been found who used the blade and burin tools of the Magdalenians of western Europe, as well as antler, bone and ivory artefacts, including eyed needles to sew skin clothing and articles of personal adornments, and who lived in huts which were partially underground, approached by entrance passages.

From Siberia the first emigrants to North America arrived, to found the prehistory of the New World. The American Indians, despite their hooked noses, have definite Mongol physical traits. In central Siberia there are people living today who are almost indistinguishable from them, with similar hair, skin colour and skeletal characteristics, so they must have migrated to America before the present characteristics, of the Mongols were fully developed. The American Indians also have certain characteristics of the Alpine race, particularly in the formation of the jaw. so it would seem that the first inhabitants of America were a mixture of primitive Mongols from Asia and Alpines from central Asia, with the Mongol strain predominating.

The Eskimos were a later arrival from Siberia and within living memory, around the northern shores of Hudson Bay and the coast of Labrador they were using weapons and implements remarkably similar to those of the Magdalenians. Their fishing spears, spear throwers, fish hooks and ice chisels of reindeer horn bear a marked resemblance to those made by the Magdalenians, as well as their harpoons, arrow-straighteners, arrowheads, personal ornaments and hairpins, all of which are beautifully carved and often decorated with incised drawings of animals and hunters. They have needles, thimbles, buttons, cups and plates of horn or ivory, and their carved animals, in walrus ivory and bone, of whales, seals and bears, are astonishingly similar in style and workmanship to the horse, mammoth and musk-ox carving of the Magdalenians.

In Europe the increasing warmth made the arctic, hunting culture of the Magdalenians gradually obsolete, and as new techniques and ways of living developed, with the changing environment and new generations of immigrants, it collapsed.

CHAPTER FOUR

The Middle Stone Age

With the end of the last phase of the Ice Age, about ten thousand years ago, the changing climate produced profound alterations in the living conditions of the people of Europe, North Africa, the eastern Mediterranean and western Asia, which were ultimately to result in the establishment of the first settled, agricultural communities, in place of the old, nomadic hunting groups, and the beginning of the New Stone Age, with its mixed farming and domesticated animals.

But the process was gradual. For the next two thousand years people were living in a transitional stage, which has been called the Mesolithic or Middle Stone Age. In some parts of the world they were experimenting with agriculture but continued their hunting life. Elsewhere, hunting was still the only source of livelihood.

In North Africa and western Asia the climate became increasingly arid, so that in a comparatively short space of time the steppe lands, including the Sahara, which had supported game for food, turned to the deserts, with their scattered oases, which exist there today; but in Europe living conditions grew pleasanter, as the ice melted and the bleak tundras gave place to forests and woodlands.

In northern Europe, at the end of the Old Stone Age, the tremendous weight of ice had pressed the land down. As the ice began to melt, pouring water into the Baltic hollow, only the higher land stood above sea level and it would have been possible to sail northwards over Lapland to the Arctic Ocean and south through a wide channel to the North Sea, but gradually the removal of the weight of the ice caused the land to rise. Lapland, southern Sweden and Denmark emerged, and the Baltic hollow became the vast Ancylus lake, so called from the tiny shells of the fresh and brackish water mollusc *ancylus fluviatilis* found in the deposits it laid down. And all the time the climate was growing milder. First willows, then birch and hazel, and finally forests of pine began to grow, and northern Europe became another possible home for mankind.

Immigrants crossed over the land-bridge of Denmark and southern Sweden and made their way in dug-out canoes—the first known water-craft—through the marshes and fens which were later to become the North Sea. Implements and weapons of these people have been found throughout northern Germany, Denmark, southern Sweden and the countries surrounding the Baltic, and it seems likely that they came from north-western Asia.

An important discovery of their industries was made in the moors at Mullerup, on the west coast of Zealand, and they have been called the Maglemoseans—the People of the Big Bog. They were hunters, fishers and fowlers, subsisting on the fish of the Ancylus lake and the surrounding waterways, and living mostly on rafts of pine and birch branches moored in shallow waters near the lake shores or in the marshes. They made their way to Britain, and one of their canoes has been found near the river Tay at Perth. Not long ago a bone prong of one of their fishing spears was dragged up in a fisherman's net off the Norfolk coast, and a dug-out canoe found in Holland has been carbon-dated to about 6250 B.C.

In Britain they occupied the river valleys and plains of the east coast, for this area, with the marshes covered now by the North Sea, the north German plain and the western shores of the Ancylus lake, formed the heart of their territory, but as the ice sheets retreated still further, leaving more habitable land, they reached as far as Ulster in the west, the forests of Russia in the east and Norway in the north.

Like other Mesolithic Europeans, they used minute 'pygmy' flints which they mounted in rows with resin on bone or wooden handles for arrows and spears. They also had a blunt-ended arrow for killing birds and small animals with pelts that they wished to preserve; their wooden bows were carefully made, with hand grips. They had spears mounted with antler or bone-barbed heads for hunting the wild ox, elk, stag, red and roe deer and

49

wild pigs of the forests, and for fresh-water fishing they used barbed or plain fish-hooks and lines, as well as barbed fishing spears, and also nets made from bark fibre, with sinkers and floats of tree bark.

Their flint implements consisted of scrapers and picks and a special form of chipped-axe which they used for felling trees, hollowing out their canoes and making the paddles. These wood-cutting tools were at first made from a flint core but later they were replaced by more efficient forms made from a flake with a wide cutting edge, which was fixed to a bone or wooden handle.

Tree-felling was limited to their few needs, but it was the beginning of the forest clearance which was to come when the knowledge and practice of agriculture eventually reached them.

The Maglemoseans did not continue the traditions of the late Palaeolithic artists, but they decorated their tools and other objects with engraved geometric patterns and small, circular pittings made with fine, flint awls, and they engraved animal and human figures on pendants and similar small ornaments, which may have been used as amulets, as well as carving small lumps of amber into animal forms.

In western Europe, life for the surviving Magdalenians had become increasingly difficult with the retreat of the ice, for the herds of game which had provided so abundant and easily accessible a supply of food were replaced by the solitary animals —the red deer, roedeer, wild oxen and boars—which were infinitely more difficult to pursue and capture and for which they had no adequate weapons.

A few Magdalenians lingered on in France, their arctic culture too specialised for them to be able to take advantage of the improving environment. They were a declining race of cave dwellers who lived by fishing, hunting small game and collecting berries and roots. In a cave near the little hamlet of Mas d'Azil, on the French side of the Pyrenees, some sixty miles from Toulouse, were found many Magdalenian remains, and above them those of a people with a different tool-making technique, who have been called the Azilians. There being no mammoth ivory or reindeer horn available for them by this time, the Azilians made points and harpoons of stag's horn, pierced at the base for attachment to a haft. Nearly all the harpoons were barbed on both sides and they were flatter than those of the Magdalenians, but probably derived from them. The flint work consisted of rather poorly-made gravers and chisels, awls and scrapers, all of which were used for the manufacture of their horn weapons.

The Azilians did not spread far, living mainly in the region of the Pyrenees in northern Spain and in parts of south-western France. They may have reached Switzerland and certain finds from Belgium and Britain have been claimed as Azilian, where remains of this type have been found in south-west Scotland, in Oban and on the island of Oronsay, but they may also have lived along the coasts of Wales and south-west England, on shores which have since been submerged by the sea.

In Britain, as elsewhere in Europe, these people eked out a poor sort of life collecting shell-fish and sea-birds eggs along the coasts, occasionally engaging in sea-fishing and sometimes venturing inland to hunt deer, boar and small game and collect nuts, berries and fruit.

On some of their camp sites numbers of small, water-worn rounded river pebbles have been discovered, mostly of quartzite, which were painted in simple geometric designs with red ochre, the devices consisting of circular spots, parallel straight lines, crosses or signs like the F, E and I of the alphabet. They could have been counters for a game or sacred symbols endowed with some magical power. The patterns are reminiscent of those painted on the Australian aborigines' churingas—stone or wooden discs, the abode of the owner's spirit, and the sign of the totem of the clan to which the owner belongs.

Some of the Azilian pebbles have been deliberately broken in half, which again is a widespread primitive custom. In early Egyptian tombs flint implements have been found ceremoniously broken—their 'life' removed, like that of the dead man.

The Azilians continued the Magdalenian habit of personal adornment, making necklaces and other ornaments of shells and perforated animal teeth. They also seem to have domesticated the dog to help them on their hunting expeditions, but their culture was not well adapted to the forest environment in which they found themselves, and they showed less enterprise than the Maglemoseans, with their canoes and tree-felling.

Living in Europe at the same time as the Azilians and the Maglemoseans was another group of people, who seem to have arrived, through Spain and France, from the increasing aridity of North Africa.

During Upper Palaeolithic times there was a trend towards the making of very small flint implements which culminated in the 'pygmy' industries of many of the Middle Stone Age people. These microliths, some little more than a centimetre in length, were of various shapes—triangles, crescents and trapezia. They were inserted in rows into shafts of bone or wood and held in place with resin, producing weapons with saw-like edges which were extremely sharp and efficient. The same idea was used till the present century in many parts of the Pacific. The Gilbert islanders, for example, made swords by binding a row of shark's teeth to either side of a wooden blade.

Microliths have been found in many parts of Europe and western Asia, and from the large deposits found at Fère-en-Tardenois, in north-eastern France, the people associated with them have been called Tardenoisians.

The Tardenoisians roamed over much of western Europe, reaching Britain from northern France and Belgium. Having devised no effective weapon for cutting down the forest trees, they, like the Azilians and unlike the Maglemoseans, were limited to the shores, but they also ventured on to the downlands and uplands of the Pennines to hunt game, with their hunting dogs.

After the rising of the land in northern Europe, with the melting of the ice and the removal of its enormous weight, the sea level began once more to rise and the land correspondingly to sink, as happened in every interglacial period, when the vast quantities of water which had been locked up in the ice were released Thus the lands surrounding the Baltic gradually sank in the south. About eight thousand years ago the sea flowed in to form the North Sea. It flowed through the narrow channels of the Skagerrak and Kattegart, turning the fresh water Ancylus lake into the Baltic Sea. It overran the plains of southern England and enlarged the estuaries. Drowning the connexions with Europe, the English Channel was formed and Britain was cut off from the mainland of Europe, with its scattered population of Maglemoseans, Azilians and Tardenoisians. A reasoned guess at the population figure of Britain about this time is ten thousand, living in small hunting groups of not more than twenty-five people, representing four or five families.

The climate of Britain changed again with the changes in sea level. Instead of the dry, warm summers and cold winters characteristic of a continental climate, Britain became much wetter, with south-west winds bringing in rain from the Atlantic, and in place of the pine and birch forests grew dense forests and woods of oak and beech, lime, elm and alder.

The primitive inhabitants of Britain, still hunters and food-gatherers, began to build the first small dwellings in the island, simple shelters scooped a foot or two down below ground level and roofed with boughs and sods of earth.

The shores of the Baltic abounded in oysters, mussels, cockles and periwinkles, and people living near the water's edge ate them in thousands. Piles of discarded shells have been found, forming huge mounds sometimes a hundred and fifty metres long, twenty metres wide and five metres high. These gigantic dustbins were the refuse from the Baltic kitchens, and industries found with them have been called 'Kitchen Midden'. A few burials of these people have been found, but they tell very little. Sometimes the body was surrounded by a few large stones, but usually it was laid in the ground with no ceremony.

The Kitchen Midden people made stone and bone implements similar to those of the Maglemoseans—scrapers, picks and boring instruments in stone, as well as axe-heads and arrowheads, with bone implements mostly from stags' antlers. They used less decoration than the Maglemoseans, but occasionally incised simple patterns on their bone implements.

Nevertheless there are signs in the Kitchen Midden culture of an advance towards the tremendous changes which were about to take place throughout the Old World with the beginning of the New Stone Age. They made an early crude form of pottery, an art which they had probably learnt through contact with the people of the dawning New Stone Age in the Near East.

No one knows just how pottery came to be made. Men and women must have devised some method of carrying things before this time, probably a simple net bag of vegetable fibres for such things as oysters and a skin bag for water. They must have hit on the idea of lining a net bag with clay, to make it stronger and water-tight, and this theory is supported by the fact that some of the earliest pottery bears marks of fibre string. From lining a bag with clay it is a very short step to making a complete clay vessel.

The pots of the Kitchen Midden people were very rough and the bases rounded or pointed, which meant that they had to be pressed into the ground to be kept upright.

Contemporary with the Kitchen Midden people were the Asturians of northern Spain and eastern Portugal, whose remains have been found above those of the Azilians, in caves and rock shelters throughout the Asturias and along the coasts, where their refuse heaps, chiefly composed of shells, are still to be found. Like the Baltic Kitchen Midden people, they lived mainly on shell fish, and vast quantities were thrown into the caves, the piles of débris in some cases reaching nearly to the roofs.

Although they were surrounded by horses, pigs and oxen, the Asturians did not succeed in domesticating them nor did they make pottery, their crafts being restricted to stone and bone artefacts, which included picks, rubbers and boring instruments.

Another group of people living towards the end of the Middle Stone Age or the early years of the New Stone Age were found at Campigny in Normandy. They lived in small huts, the floors of which were dug a metre or so below ground level, and their implements were similar to those of the Kitchen Midden people— roughly shaped stone picks, axes, arrowheads, awls and scrapers —and a little crude pottery has been found.

Life was still primitive and in western Europe there had been little advance in material culture and comfort since the close of the Old Stone Age, but the ancestors of the three main races of Europe, the Alpines, the Mediterraneans and the Nordics, were already established and the stage was set for the rapid development of civilisation which was about to take place, following the birth of the New Stone Age. This came about with the practice of agriculture and the domestication of animals, with the attendant skills of farming, the knowledge of which gradually spread westwards from the eastern Mediterranean and western Asia, where it all began.

CHAPTER FIVE

The New Stone Age

When the first farmers discovered the processes of agriculture and adopted them as a principal means of livelihood it brought about the most profound change in their lives that mankind had ever experienced. From hunters and food gatherers, who of necessity lived in small groups and covered large distances in the course of their lives, in the enternal quest for food, they were able to settle down and establish themselves in communities. They were no longer nomads, wresting a subsistence where they could find it. They had a measure of stability, and the knowledge that they could produce their own food supply gave them an added confidence which released new emotions and new skills, resulting in rapid cultural advances which were soon to develop into the first civilisations.

They now felt that life depended on spiritual forces to which hitherto they had paid little regard—the fertility of the earth, the warmth of the sun and the beneficence of rain—and new gods and goddesses were conceived, to be worshipped, feared and placated.

By about 8000 B.C. several agricultural settlements had come into existence in the crescent of land stretching from the Nile delta through Palestine and Syria to the foothills of Turkey and northern Iraq, southern Iran, the Caspian and Turkestan. This was where the spread of desert conditions in post-glacial times made the old hunting life increasingly difficult. Unlike the inhabitants of western Europe, where game and fish were abundant and people had no need to change their hunting ways, the people of these arid regions were forced to look for alternative sources of food. They were fortunate, for it was in this part of the world alone that the 'noble grasses', barley and wheat, grew wild, their indigenous distribution being restricted to the area between the Adriatic and the Caspian Sea: and it was here that the earliest agricultural communities arose.

The earliest form of food production was more akin to horticulture than agriculture, and in the first place it would have been the work of women, a continuation of their daily labour of digging for roots and gathering wild fruit and berries, while the men were away on their hunting expeditions. And it was probably women who, first noticing that seeds falling on the ground reproduced themselves, began the early experiments in agriculture.

When women began to produce this valuable food it added greatly to their social importance, for they became the stable element in a previously nomadic society. Early argricultural communities recognised the right of a family group to till its own chosen plot of land and reap the rewards, and the women may have been the first to assert this right, to the point where the system of matriarchy was devised, the primitive social organisation in which women are regarded as the owners of the land, and its inheritance is through the female line. Agriculture certainly brought about a profound change in religious concepts, for now all the mysteries of reproduction were focused in the goddess of the earth—the Great Mother Goddess.

Later, as agriculture became increasingly important in the economy, and labours were first shared and eventually taken over almost entirely by husbands and sons, men were duly appointed to their rightful position in the hierarchy of the gods. The Mother Goddess was given a son and a lover who, in the end, entirely usurped her position of supremacy.

Evidence of the first domestication of animals is not so clear as that of the first agriculture. The wild ox ranged widely throughout Europe and Asia, in a broad band of distribution from Britain to North Africa in the west, stretching eastwards, north of the Himalayas to the Pacific coast; and the wild pig was found in most parts of Europe and in many parts of southern Asia: but wild sheep and goats were limited in their range, found most commonly in western Asia, where the wheat and barley grew. As the patches of grain ripened, they must have been a temptation to the wild animals, and as these animals foraged amongst the crops it is easy to see how, with the help of the dog, which had already been domesticated in the hunting days, they were gradually tamed and brought into use not only for their meat, but also for their wool, skins and milk.

In Palestine as early as the eighth millennium B.C. people were living in settlements of small, sunken houses and cultivating cereals, although they had not yet succeeded in domesticating animals. A remarkable sequence of events has been unearthed at the oasis of Jericho, where layer after layer of the twenty-four metre high tell have been excavated, reaching down to bedrock and the remains of people who were living there nine or ten thousand years ago.

These were Mesolithic hunting and fishing folk, the Natufians, a small group of families who were camping on the site, probably in cave shelters, round the waters of Jordan. They lived mainly by hunting the gazelle, but they also harvested wild grain with reaping knives inset with flint blades. They had no storage bins, so far as one can tell, and still lived the hand-to-mouth existence of primitive food-gatherers, but above this Natufian layer, which has been radio-carbon dated to 7800 B.C., were the remains of a people with more permanent settlements, who were moving into a Neolithic culture. Their numbers had increased and they lived in beehive-shaped huts of mud brick, with sunken floors and sloping walls. Their flint implements included ground stone-axes, and there is evidence that they were having success with their experiments in the cultivation of cereals.

Their treatment of the dead was curious. Before burial, the head was severed from the body and heads were buried separately, in nests. A similar custom was found in Europe, where at Ofnet, in southern Germany, a cache of severed heads was found in Mesolithic levels.

This early Jericho, large enough to contain three thousand inhabitants, was surrounded by the first town wall yet discovered, a massive structure with round towers set at intervals, approached by inner stairways and flanked by a ditch cut from the solid rock, three metres deep and nine metres across at the top.

By about 6000 B.C. Jericho was inhabited by people who were living in brick-built houses with rectangular rooms grouped round a central courtyard. The walls and floors were covered with plaster, which was burnished with polishing stones until it was almost waterproof, and they buried their dead under the house floors, with great care and ceremony, still removing the skull but often filling it with plaster and modelling a plaster portrait over the facial bones, with shells inserted in the eye sockets, creating startlingly realistic personal representations, similar to those which were to be made of the Egyptian Pharaohs in the years to come.

These early inhabitants of Jericho still had no pottery, but they were using wooden or stone bowls and also goat-skin bottles and platters of woven grass. They do not seem to have cultivated grain yet, but their stone reaping knives with their serrated edges suggest that they were gathering the wild grain for food, like their predecessors.

The settlement was surrounded by an even stronger stone wall than the earlier one, made from boulders carried from the mountains half a mile away.

After this time, Jericho seems to have been inhabited by a barbarian, peasant people who had no houses but lived in tents, but in this level Jericho's first pottery is found— a cream ware with a polished red decoration—and by 4500 B.C. Neolithic people were occupying the site with a fully established pottery industry, and using tools and weapons of stone and flint which included knives, chisels and sickle blades for cutting grain.

Similar settlements to Jericho, though not telling so complete a story, have been found at Jarmo, in the Kurdish foothills of northern Iraq. Here the remains of mud brick houses built on stone foundations were discovered. The rooms were rectangular and the floors covered with reed mats. Stone implements found with them included reaping knives with serrated edges formed by microliths, polished stone-axes, pestles, mortars and milling stones for their grain. They seem to have kept herds of sheep, goats, cattle and pigs, but although the site is dated to about 4500 B.C. they had not yet acquired the art of making pottery.

A full Neolithic culture usually comprised the four important skills of agriculture, the domestication of animals, a technique of flint and stone working by pressure and polishing and the making of pottery, but people did not necessarily acquire all four arts at the same time.

Pottery seems to have first been made towards the end of the sixth millennium B.C., and its earliest appearance was in this region of south-western Asia. It occurs in the border country of western Syria and Turkey, from where the knowledge must have drifted down to Jericho, in northern Iraq and eastern Syria, and on the plateau of Iran. These early pots were very simple, with a small mouth, but they were sometimes decorated with an incised geometric pattern.

In western Syria the pots were made by a farming people who lived in groups of rectangular-roomed houses which formed the nucleus of settlement tells. They used reaping knives, polished stone-axes and tanged lanceheads, and they were beginning to weave flax and wool.

In northern Iraq people were practising a very similar kind of culture, and there they developed a high skill in pottery which, though still hand made, was excellently fired and beautifully decorated with red, yellow, orange and black paint on a cream slip. At first the patterns were geometric but later they developed into stylised representations of men and animals, particularly bulls. As well as pots, they made dishes, flasks and bowls with hollowed pedestals. They used obsidian as well as stone for their implements, which included tanged, projectile heads, and occasionally they made beads and similar ornaments from local surface finds of copper—the first step towards a metal age.

Their worship of the Mother Goddess and her consort manifested itself in their clay figurines of women, with large breasts and exaggerated buttocks, and they also made models in clay, bone and stone of the farmyard animals, especially the bulls, which may have been amulets.

These people, the Halafians, were the ancestors of the Assyrians, and their bull cult was already emerging.

On the Iranian plateau there were similar communities, subsisting on mixed farming, and making their first experiments in metallurgy, with the hammering of copper pins and awls. Excavations near Persepolis revealed crude, hand-made plain pottery in the lowest levels, associated with a well-developed stone industry and numerous bone tools. Farther north, on the eastern slopes of the mountains forming the western rim of the Iranian desert, a camp site was found and above it mud huts whose inhabitants had used reaping knives and were engaged in mixed farming, with agriculture and domesticated cattle and sheep. They made several kinds of hand-made pottery, which was at first undecorated, but in later levels they were producing buff coloured pottery decorated with black paint, red, oxidised pottery, at first plain but later decorated in black, and a little all-black pottery. Their stone work bore traces of mesolithic ancestry and included microliths and slotted, bone-reaping knives, with handles ending in carved animal heads. They had no clay figurines and they buried their dead somewhat casually, between the houses, with no separate cemetery.

Iran was becoming increasingly arid and the climate was too dry for a civilization to develop which could be in any way comparable with those which were about to dawn in the river valleys of the Tigris, the Euphrates and the Nile, but it was from the Iranian plateau and the highlands of the west and south-west, that the first colonisers made their way down the Tigris valley, searching for new lands. They were Neolithic farmers with domesticated animals, a knowledge of agriculture and pottery and a high degree of skill in stone-working. They also had the beginnings of a knowledge of metallurgy, though as yet they used only copper and then only for personal trinkets. These colonists finally settled in the fertile land between the Tigris and the Euphrates of southern Iraq, the land which was later to be called Babylon and which the Greeks called Mesopotamia, the land between the two rivers.

These were the Ubaid people, who took their name from the low tell not far from the ancient site of Ur, where much of the knowledge of their culture was unearthed, and they laid the foundations of the first historic civilisation of Mesopotamia—that of the Sumerians.

Despite the rivers, the land was unpromising desert which needed to be irrigated, yet it proved a challenge to men who had already accumulated a fund of knowledge and skills. Their first settlements were small villages built of whatever material came to hand, the earliest houses consisting merely of reed mats hung between palm stems and plastered with mud, but soon they were using sun-dried clay bricks and later still kiln-dried bricks, more expensive and used only for the more important buildings, but more durable, for sun-dried brick buildings usually collapsed after being inhabited for two or three generations and were re-built on the same site, thus producing the characteristic tells.

These Ubaid people, peasant farmers with domestic livestock, also hunted and fished in the marshes and rivers. They made boats from bundles of reeds and had soon invented a slow-moving wheel for their pottery. By 4350 B.C. they had spread over the whole of Iraq, absorbing the Halafians occupying the northern part of the country, and their scattered villages were tending to form themselves into groups with a specific centre, which were to develop into the city states of their great civilisation.

During these years the Neolithic arts were spreading westwards into Egypt, eastwards to the Indus valley and northwards to Europe.

In Europe progress was slow and the processes of diffusion complicated. As late as the second millennium B.C. there were parts of northern Europe and Asia where agriculture had not yet been adopted and people were still living in the hunting and fishing communities of Palaeolithic and Mesolithic times, but elsewhere the knowledge gradually spread, coming in the first place from the Near East by way of north Greece and the Balkans to the plains of the Danube and Hungary. By about 5000 B.C. an agricultural peasantry was established here which persisted with relatively little change for the next three thousand years, for although it could be described as a western province of the peasant culture of the Near East, it was on the far periphery and, for a long time to come, was little affected by the developments at the heart.

The peasants of Bulgaria, Thessaly and Macedonia, whose settlements became tells like those of the East, lived in villages of widely scattered, single-roomed huts which were made from a light wooden frame filled in with wattle and daub, but unlike the eastern dwellings, the roofs were gabled, a necessary adaptation to the climate. In early days, the houses were square, but by about 3000 B.C. or 2000 B.C. the plan had changed. Houses were rectangular and furnished with a porch. The walls were plastered and painted with decorative patterns and the villagers were beginning to import small copper trinkets.

At a site in Bulgaria, where habitation first began during the sixth millennium B.C. and continued for the next three thousand years, clay models of chairs and benches were found among the fifty to sixty houses which formed the village, and it has been calculated that each household of say five people farmed about seven acres of land.

The pottery of the Danubian peasants was in the Eastern tradition and included small amulets in the form of stamp seals, many female figurines and a few animal figures. The settlements in the tells were permanent and a clear indication that agriculture was practised in east-central Europe, as far as the region of Budapest, by about 5000 B.C.

Soon after this time farming communities were established farther west, on the loess soil of central Europe, reaching Czechoslovakia, Germany and the southern Netherlands within the next five hundred years.

The culture of these central Europeans was remarkably uniform. Their houses were completely different from those of the east Europeans, being immensely long, gabled halls, sometimes measuring thirty metres by eight metres in depth, built with a massive timber frame and wooden walls covered with clay. They probably housed the cattle byres and storage barns as well as the extended household of parents, married sons and daughters and their children; and villages might consist of twenty or more of these 'long houses'.

As the families established themselves in their new settlements, they had to clear the ground of a certain amount of vegetation, even on the open parkland, and this was accomplished by cutting and burning. They had no ploughs yet and their cultivation was still with the digging stick and hoe. They kept their cattle pasturage to a minimum and concentrated on growing grain.

After seven or eight years, as the ground became exhausted, the household would abandon its plot and move on, but later generations often returned, after the soil was regenerated, and rebuilt the old homesteads.

Their domesticated animals included cows, pigs, goats and sheep, which were probably tethered by day and brought into the house at night. They grew wheat and barley and also beans, peas, lentils and flax. Although the countryside abounded in game, they seem to have largely disregarded it, for little hunting equipment is found among their remains and hardly any bones of game. They used stone adze blades and the women made simple, rounded pots, some of which were decorated with incised linear and spiral patterns.

The villages were fenced as a protection from marauding wild animals, but there is no evidence that these people possessed any military weapons. They appear to have been an essentially peaceful people with no ruling families or class distinctions, and members of the widely scattered villages visited each other in friendliness, perhaps travelling by river through the oak forests.

It seems that it was only with human aggression, in the years to come, that peasant people would choose a council of advisers from amongst the older and wiser men of the community, to advise and act in time of emergency; and when the crisis was over these men would return to their homes and their ordinary lives again. The conception of the tribal leader and an upper, ruling class came much later.

This peaceful peasant culture of central Europe which, with the natural increase of an agricultural population, gradually spread westwards and northwards over Europe, taking its Neolithic culture and peasant religion with it, was the foundation on which all later European cultures were imposed. It has persisted, with its traditions and folk-lore, throughout the long history of invaders and conquerors of varying races and languages, for language and racial terms have little significance in the essential structure of a society in which the peasants are living in a direct tradition which has lasted for more than six thousand years.

The main colonisation of northern and western Europe was by way of the Mediterranean, from the Aegean to southern Italy and then to Sicily and Spain. It began about 5000 B.C. and by 3000 B.C. the practice of agriculture had spread from southern France to Switzerland and northern Italy.

Few remains of these early agricultural settlements have been found except in Switzerland, where the evidence of lake-side villages has come to light. They were composed of small, timber-framed houses built on the damp ground close to the shores of the lakes, and by 3000 B.C. to 2000 B.C. the villages comprised anything from twenty-four to seventy-five houses, each house being about six to seven metres long by three or more metres deep, divided into two rooms and often protected by a porch.

The farming settlements of western Europe during the third millennium B.C. grew wheat, barley, peas, beans and lentils and also a small apple, which was probably used for making cider. Their cattle were tethered and stalled and fed largely on the leaves of trees. Flax was cultivated, both for its seeds and fibre, and as well as weaving linen the women made beautiful basketry.

By 3000 B.C. the inhabitants of the north European plain and southern Scandinavia had taken to farming, living in villages of up to fifty rectangular houses; and within the next few hundred years the first farmers had crossed the Channel, with their seeds of grain and their cattle and sheep, and landed in Britain. Some came from western and northern France, and more from the north European plain, and they settled on Britain's southern and eastern shores at first.

For twenty thousand years the people of Britain had been hunters and fishers. Now, with the arrival of these slender, dark-haired Mediterranean peoples, the face of the countryside slowly changed. Avoiding the dense forests of the lowlands, the new-comers moved on to the more open uplands, in time reaching the Lincolnshire wolds and Yorkshire, the lowlands of Scotland and north-western Ireland. For the first time in its history small plots of corn appeared on the English countryside, cultivated by the women with their digging sticks and hoes, and flocks and herds grazed on the hillsides.

People banded together to form small settlements. Some of these villages were entrenched by ditches and earthworks, prob-ably, in the first place, as a defence against wild animals. Throughout southern England, from Devon to Sussex, the remains of several of these encampments have survived, mostly on the chalk downs. The largest is on the summit of Windmill hill, near Avebury, in Wiltshire, and these first British farmers have been named after it the Windmill Hill people.

At the Windmill Hill village several concentric rings of ditches with wide spaces in between were dug around the central site. The earth from the ditches was piled along the inner ridge to form a high bank, which may have been reinforced with a stock-ade. The ditches were not continuous, but divided into segments by solid causeways of untouched earth, which were probably left to give easy access for the animals when they were brought in for safety.

Camps of this kind are known archaeologically as 'causeway camps'. At Windmill Hill there is no evidence that people lived in the centre of the camp, as one might have supposed. Their remains have been found in the shelter of the embankments and it seems likely that, at this stage, places like Windmill Hill were used only temporarily, perhaps in the autumn, when the cattle and sheep were brought in for branding and gelding. Away from these camps there must have been many isolated settlements, such as the round huts of Cornwall and the rectangular house, built on a stone foundation, which was found in Devon.

The domesticated cattle of early Neolithic Britain were a fair-sized breed with spreading horns, but a large number were probably wasted each year by being killed off when the grass crop failed in the late autumn, a wastage which continued all through the Middle Ages and lingered on until the early eighteenth century, when with the important agricultural innovations of Jethro Tull and Lord 'Turnip' Townshend, turnips and other root crops were grown more extensively for winter cattle feed.

Most Neolithic households kept pigs, which were sent down to the forested valleys to feed on acorns. The hunters of venison, birds and other small game used arrows tipped with small, leaf-shaped flint heads in their bows and the women made pottery by hand—mostly round-bottomed bowls and jars, plain but very fine and beautifully shaped, with only occasionally a little impressed decoration. There is no evidence that they had acquired a knowledge of weaving yet, so their clothing probably consisted of furs and garments of leather.

Of their work in wood practically nothing survives, but they must have attained a fair degree of competency in order to make their axe-shafts, clubs, paddles, fishing tridents, dug-out canoes and house frames.

Their output of flint implements was enormous, varying from the universal scrapers to the delicately made arrowheads, while their heavy, ground and polished flint-axes, adzes and picks were probably the work of specialists, for they seem to have become articles of barter, being made from a special kind of stone which was not available in all parts of the country. Axes made from a particularly hard stone from North Wales, for example, have been found in South Wales, Wessex and as far east as Essex.

Already they had to mine for their flint and several pits have been found in the chalk of southern and eastern England up to twelve metres deep, often with a complicated network of underground galleries and tunnels. The most famous flint mines are at Grimes' Graves near Brandon in Norfolk, where a tradition of flint knapping, begun nearly five thousand years ago, continued until the present century, for the knappers of Brandon were still making flints for export to Africa until the 1960s, when the last of the flint-lock guns were still in use.

The Neolithic flint miners worked by the light of chalk lamps, with wicks floating in oil. Their shovels were the scapulae of animals, their picks, hammers and wedges were antlers. The knappers worked at the pit-head, leaving behind them piles of débris and wasters (i.e., spoilt flints).

In the depths of one of the pits at Grimes' Graves, close to a gallery entrance, was found on a pedestal of chalk blocks the carved chalk figure, about ten centimetres high, of a grotesque, pregnant woman looking down at a phallus, and at her feet, on a triangular platform of flints, seven deer antlers had been laid. These were probably offerings to the Mother Goddess by miners who had run into trouble, for the shaft where they had been working had proved to be unusually poor in its yield of flints.

This is the most important piece of evidence of the religious beliefs of the Windmill Hill people. Elsewhere there is little to be found. Often the treatment of their dead was casual, for bones have been found tipped without care into the ground. There are examples of individual burials, often near the site of a dwelling house, the body having been placed in a specially constructed grave, sometimes lined with blocks of stone or chalk, but with few if any grave goods.

However, their best known burial sites are the long, earth barrows mostly to be found in Wessex and Sussex, near the flint mines and causewayed camps, and on the chalk uplands of Lincolnshire and Yorkshire.

These large, earthen mounds were sometimes more than a hundred metres long and sixteen metres wide, and at Maiden Castle in Dorset, where an Iron Age camp was later to be built, there is a Neolithic barrow more than half a kilometre in length.

The barrow was surrounded by a ditch, which supplied the material for the mound, and it was usually U-shaped and higher at one end than the other. The burial chamber inside was roughly rectangular, supported by wooden posts and clods of earth. Here up to twenty-five bodies might be buried, although in some the remains of only one have been found. The bodies seem to have been reduced to skeletons before interment and often the bones are in disorder, which suggests that they had been previously buried in some mortuary house and at a later date transferred to the barrow for a mass interment, after which the barrow was permanently sealed.

Bodies were mostly buried in the crouched position, but in Yorkshire and Westmorland have been found barrows with multiple burials, where the bodies were cremated in specially dug trenches during the construction of the barrow.

With the Mediterranean stream of influence which brought the Neolithic arts and crafts to northern and western Europe came also the practice of building monumental tombs. The precise religious motivation for building these megalithic monuments is obscure, but it was part of the universal desire amongst people of the ancient world to preserve the life of the departed for a continued existence in the next world. This megalithic culture reached France, the British Isles and the Baltic from the Atlantic coast of Spain, where it had arrived from the eastern Mediterranean. Megalithic building also spread eastwards, though probably at a later date, from Egypt to Palestine, India and the Pacific, and the prototype of the magalithic tomb may well have been the Egyptian mastaba, a representation of the earthly home of the deceased.

In Europe many of these graves have survived, in varying degrees of preservation, some five thousand having been recorded in France, three thousand in the Danish islands and nearly two thousand in the British Isles.

There is a great deal of variation in the plan, which suggests that once the idea of building some massive burial monument was accepted, people adapted it in various ways, according to the material available and their individual tastes. Nevertheless, there are two basic types, both of which are to be found in Britain, the passage grave, with an approach passage leading to an approximately circular burial chamber, and the gallery grave, which had no approach passage but a formal entrance, sometimes in the form of a massive lintel supported by two stone columns, giving directly on to a rectangular burial chamber, often with pillared recesses along both sides, for the reception of the bodies. These chambered tombs were made for a succession of burials and were in the nature of family vaults. Some were in continuous use for a thousand years, and they were still being built as late as 1500 B.C.

There is a large group of gallery graves in the Cotswolds, where huge cairns of stones heaped over burial chambers formed from massive blocks of stone resemble in shape the earthen long barrows of the Windmill Hill people. One of the most famous is Hetty Pegler's Tump, a strange, artificial cave approached by a low stone porth, composed of a heavy lintel supported by two upright stone blocks, leading to a long chamber with cells opening on either side, between massive stone pillars, where the bodies were placed with offerings of personal ornaments, weapons and pottery vessels for food and drink. After the interment the

67

entrance was carefully sealed until the time came for the next burial, with all its attendant rituals.

There are numbers of these graves in the west of England and a few occur farther east, notably Wayland's Smithy, near Lambourn, on the Berkshire downs, though the legend of Wayland Smith, the mythical blacksmith who would shoe a horse if a groat were left on top of the smithy, and would take offence if more money were offered, belongs to some time in the Iron Age, which did not begin in Britain until about 500 B.C.

Most of the megalithic tombs of Britain are found near the west coast and the western river estuaries and as far north as the Hebrides, the Shetlands and the Orkneys, with an important group in Ireland. This suggests that the cult was brought to Britain by seafarers who had made their way from the Mediterranean and the Atlantic and then sailed northwards through the Irish Sea. After about 2300 B.C. it is possible to trace a sequence of this megalithic tomb building throughout Sicily, Sardinia, southern France, Spain and Portugal, then in Brittany and Britain, and finally on the shores of the Baltic.

Little is known of the religious cult associated with the megalithic monuments nor of the people who introduced the practice of building them, but they were probably the first explorers and speculators, forerunners of the later metal traders. Some of the megaliths are carved with patterns derived from a highly stylised representation of animal and human forms, which had undoubtedly some symbolical and magical or religious significance.

The megalith builders who arrived in Ireland seem to have been the first metal and gold prospectors, and from Ireland they reached Scotland, to establish the first trade in copper. Others colonised the Western Isles, some sailing round the north of Scotland to Scandinavia.

In addition to the Windmill Hill peasants, with their causewayed camps and long earth barrows, and the megalith builders who followed them, the descendants of the old Mesolithic inhabitants of Britain—the Peterborough people—still survived in the eastern part of the country for a time but ultimately were integrated into the rest of the population.

CHAPTER SIX

Primitive Peoples and Civilisation

The first civilisations came about when men began to live in permanent settlements, with a social and religious structure, a written language and a specialisation of employments, made possible by the surplus of food produced by the mass of basic peasant farmers, which resulted in the creation of a class system.

This change from barbarism to civilisation had a profound effect on the character of mankind. Until this time there is little or no evidence that men behaved in an aggressive or violent way towards each other. On the contrary, there is a mass of information to be found in the accounts of civilised observers of historical times, who visited peoples still living in a state of stone-age hunting savagery, to show that human beings in a primitive state are instinctively friendly and amiable beings. It is a standard of behaviour which can be called human nature and it is reasonable to suppose that men and women behaved in this way throughout the long years of the Stone Age. They were peaceful, fair-minded and honest, and they maintained these ethical virtues until the fear of aggression and the injustices of civilisation forced them to the realisation that they must defend themselves.

In historical times, the records of travellers visiting peoples untouched by civilisation show a remarkable consistency when describing their behaviour. Early in the present century the Veddahs of Ceylon, for example, were found living in rock shelters, in communities of relatives, each community having its own hunting ground. They were peaceful, courteous, truthful, strictly monogamous and had a high standard of marital fidelity.

Men and women shared the same food, living on equal terms in every respect, and they were affectionate and indulgent parents.

The Semang of the Malay Peninsula were food-gathering tribes living in a state of social equality, with communal property. They were monogamous, observing the marital tie faithfully, and murder, theft and drunkenness were unknown among them.

The Sakai tribes of Malaya had no warfare or inter-tribal fighting. They were described as simple, kind-hearted, upright, truthful and scrupulously just. They were mainly monogamous, though a few had adopted polygamy.

The Andamanese of the Andaman Islands lived in settled villages, each family to a hut, though formerly they had lived in communal huts. They had no organised government but a great respect for seniority, as well as for the qualities of generosity, kindness and freedom from bad temper. They do not seem to have had any concept of the punishment of crime, and when quarrels arose there would be a good deal of hard swearing, and sometimes a man would work himself up into a high pitch of anger, and seize his bow and fire an arrow at a spot near the other disputant, or vent his ill-temper by destroying any property he could lay his hands on. It would, however, need only the slightest show of authority by a third person to end such a dispute.

Divorce was rare and polygamy unknown, and the very young, the weak, the aged, and the helpless, were made special objects of interest and attention, being better provided with the comforts and necessities of daily life than the otherwise more fortunate members of the community.

The Kubu of Sumatra were monogamous food-gatherers, living in family groups, a peaceful, rather shy people, with no social organisation.

At the beginning of the century the Punan of Borneo were perhaps the most primitive people in the world, for they had been living in isolation in the forests for centuries, ignoring the more 'sophisticated' habits of their neighbours, which included head-hunting. The Punan were found to be living in communities of some twenty or thirty men and women, with their children, and had no social organisation, although one of the older men was recognised as the leader. They had no cultivation of crops and no domesticated animals, living entirely on the animals and vegetable produce of the jungle. The authority of the leader was the authority naturally accorded to age and experience, and the superior knowledge of the tribal history and traditions that comes with age: he dispensed no substantial punishments, public opinion and tradition being, apparently, a sufficient control on the conduct of individuals among these nomadic people. Decisions on when and where to move were the result of open discussion, with the leader exercising an influence proportional to the esteem in which his knowledge and judgment were held.

The Punan were mainly monogamous and marriage was regarded as being for life. There was no polygamy but occasionally there were cases of polyandry, where a woman was married to an elderly man and had no children, but wanted some.

The Negritoes of northern Luzon, in the Philippines, were always very friendly, and appeared to consider the whole Negrito race as one large family, any member of which was always welcome to their homes, and free to hunt in their forests.

The Australian aborigines had already been subjected to outside influences when they were first observed by European anthropologists, and although they had remained food-gatherers, with no pottery, agriculture or domesticated animals, except the dog, they had a complicated social organisation. The family was the unit of society and they had no ruling classes, but the tribes had hereditary chiefs and were ruled by councils of elders.

The Arunta of central Australia were usually kindly disposed to one another, and where two tribes came into contact on the border of their territories, the same friendly behaviour was maintained. They were kind and considerate to children, carrying them when they got tired on the march, and ensuring that they always had a good share of the food. The aged and infirm, too, were treated with special kindness, and given a fair share of the food.

They were monogamous, except for some of the old men, who appropriated the girls, so that young men sometimes had to wait for several years, until a wife was available for them.

The cruel habits of the Australian aborigines, the inter-tribal feuds with organised violence, the initiation ceremonies, the violence associated with marriage and death ceremonies which were recorded in the early days of their discovery can all be traced to customs and magical beliefs derived from contact with alien peoples.

In the lands bordering the Arctic Ocean, the Lapps, though

overfond of drink, were found to be peaceful and kind, the women living together on good terms, and the Samoyedes of north-western Siberia, despite a frequent shortage of food, had no social troubles and were prepared, if necessary, to starve together.

The explorer Nansen found that the Labrador Eskimos were mainly monogamous, with no ruling classes. They lived in harmony, with communal property. Not only was warfare unknown. but there was no word for it in their language. Women and men were socially equal and they were kind and devoted parents. There was no quarrelling, and if any member of the community were deserving of reproof it was accomplished by the singing of satirical songs, for they most wisely considered that it was unnecessary for more than one person to be annoyed at a time.

The Alaskan Eskimos were very different, quarrelsome and treacherous and engaged in constant bloodshed and tribal warfare with the Dené tribes of the Athabascan basin, but there is ample proof that this behaviour had been provoked by alien contacts.

From the study of the literature describing the ways of these primitive peoples of Asia, Africa, the islands of the Pacific and the Americas it is clear that the fundamental unit of society is not the primal horde but the family, and where there is a tribal organisation, the units of which it is composed are families. These family groups lived in juxtaposition and the regulation of affairs was carried out by the elders.

Generally speaking, the marriage rule is a strict and life-long monogamy. There is an equilibrium between the sexes and harmonious behaviour within the family. Even though in some societies pre-marital sexual licence is accepted, marriage is intended to be permanent, with economic, legal and social advantages, its purpose being the establishment of a household and the producing of children with a legalised status.

The various forms of sexual licence which have existed from the dawn of history until the present day, in all civilised communities, cannot therefore be attributed to the survival of a barbaric period of promiscuity but to the habits of civilisation.

Polygamy and polyandry have never been so widespread as is often asserted, and they occur mainly where the numerical balance of the sexes has been disturbed, while it is very doubtful whether the custom of 'group marriages' ever existed at all.

Children are invariably treated kindly by their parents and

the children are good to old people. Among the Eskimos the old people were sometimes killed off, but it seems that this was probably at their own request or of necessity, through lack of food.

There is no evidence that the stronger appropriated food from the weaker, and the general characteristic was to share food, even when there was a shortage.

Hospitality is general. In regard to private property, only that which is actually used by the individual is considered private, as for example a man's hunting weapons or a woman's domestic utensils. With no instinct to acquire property, people are truthful and honest, the acquisitive instinct being a later development and a reaction to social institutions.

There is little evidence of violence among primitive people, quarrels being mainly about women and breaches of marriage. Behaviour, generally speaking, is peaceful, and this way of living has apparently come about with biological evolution.

Mankind has three innate instincts, the sex instinct which perpetuates the species, the instinct for self-preservation and the instinct to acquire food. The whole Palaeolithic industry was centred round the procuring of food, rather than fighting, and by Upper Palaeolithic times, with their cave paintings and magic ritual, it would seem that men had begun to elaborate theories of cause and effect, processes of thought which were to lead to the first religious concepts, although this intellectual activity was stimulated by the basic instinct to procure food.

Mankind had an urge to portray things, but after this was satisfied a new form of activity began to unfold for him, in which he took artistic pleasure. This may have evolved from some quality that he already possessed, or it may have been something which he created for himself.

The instinct for self-preservation was extended to the treatment of the dead. The feminine figurines of Palaeolithic times represented the life-giving functions of women: and in the tombs of the early civilisations they were found as amulets, put in the grave to help the dead, together with the red ochre which, as a substitute for blood, would serve to restore life to the body.

In the creation of religious and social organisations of all kinds, including that of the kingship, mankind has never moved very far from the three fundamental innate tendencies for food, family and self-preservation, which function all the way through society.

The kingship was a huge, magical mechanism for maintaining the prosperity of the community and was concerned with food, law and order: and the first religious systems were also largely concerned with the obtaining of food.

Although the same pattern of innate tendencies is everywhere present, the ultimate results in differing societies is by no means the same.

Primitive peoples, untouched by civilisation, did not practise the horrible habits of head-hunting, human sacrifice or cannibalism, and were never wantonly cruel. Amongst the few primitive food-gatherers who were found to indulge in organised violence, the quarrelsome Eskimos of Alaska used a plated armour which was not indigenous and had been acquired from some alien people, along with the belligerent behaviour associated with it.

Amongst the Andamanese, who in their natural state had been so amiable, survivors from all shipwrecks were always killed, but this behaviour had been induced by their sufferings at the hands of the murderous Malay pirates, who had learnt their habits from the Arabs and who affected the peoples of Borneo and the north coast of Australia. When Captain Cook visited the Tonga Islands he called them the Friendly Islands, because of the kindness of his reception. It was later, on a second visit to Hawaii, that there was a misunderstanding between his men and the natives. After a native chief had been killed by one of his officers, the natives killed Captain Cook.

In the first place, the stimulus for war may have been the necessity to procure victims for human sacrifice to the gods, in order that the well-being of the community could be maintained.

In Indonesia, head-hunting was the most frequent cause of war among certain tribes, although people such as the Iban of Borneo, who acquired the habit only in the eighteenth century, from the Malays, soon turned it into a savage and cruel sport for its own sake.

Violence once begun seems to be self-perpetuating. Among the North American Indians, after the Spaniards had reintroduced the horse, horse-stealing became an important diversion, but it soon turned to scalping, and the honours which once went to the man who had stolen the most horses went to the one who had collected the most scalps.

Many societies have practised human sacrifice and then abandoned it. The Greeks practised it in the early days of their civilisation and then relinquished it. There was usually a reason for it in the first place, people having been persuaded that it would benefit the community. Human blood, they were told, was a good fertiliser for the fields. In Mexico the sun had to be kept alive by human blood.

Cannibalism was also rationalised, a man eating another human being in order to acquire his traits of bravery and virility.

But basically these habits are repugnant to human beings, and once the theoretical core for the false interpretations of natural phenomena is forgotten, the institutions die out.

CHAPTER SEVEN

The First Great Civilisations

While Neolithic farmers were slowly colonising Europe, the first known civilisation of the world was coming into existence in Iraq, where, by 4350 B.C., the Ubaid people were beginning to form their city states. There were more than fifteen of them eventually including Erech, Lagash, Kish, Eridu and Ur, which ultimately covered a thousand hectares and had a population of some 500,000.

They were self-contained and self-governing, but economically inter-dependent. At first they were on friendly terms with each other, but later there was intense rivalry between them and wars developed.

The basis of their lives was agriculture and since this required irrigation, there was of necessity a high degree of social organisation for the cutting of the irrigation canals and their maintenance.

Barley was the main crop, but they also grew wheat, emmer wheat, millet, sesame and the date palm, as well as various fruits and vegetables, and with domesticated cattle and sheep there was an abundance of food for all.

With the development of the potter's wheel and the increased knowledge of metallurgy, a class of specialist craftsmen arose—potters, metallurgists, stone-carvers, glass workers, carpenters and masons.

Mostly, the early cult of the Mother Goddess still underlay much of their religious thinking, and from being the goddess of agriculture she became the goddess of civilised life. At Erech she was worshipped as Ishtar, the Lady of Heaven, at Nippur as the Lady of the Mountain, at Ur as the Great Lady, at Kish the

August Lady or the Lady of Birth and at Umma as the Lady of the Harvest.

In earlier times the Mother Goddess had been the goddess of the untamed wild, the virgin huntress and the mistress of the wild beasts, but with the development of agriculture she was given a lover and a son, and as the cycle of the farmer's year, the dying autumn and the rebirth of spring, became of increasing significance to the life of the people, the Sumerian religion changed. Her consort, who was also her son, became the embodiment of the corn and harvest, and the two most important festivals of the year were the annual wedding of the goddess and the god and the yearly death of the god, as he descended into the underworld.

The Sumerian city states were at first, as in all primitive societies, governed by a group of older men, but soon the function of kingship arose, the king being the supreme ruler of the state, answerable only to the god, and his most important function was to control the waters of the irrigation, by which alone the people could survive.

The office of kingship was made hereditary and each city now had its king and also its god. The early gods of the cities were now believed to have created men and kings to carry on their cities and build their temples, and the king, though bearing no relationship to the god, was considered to be under his special protection.

In Sumer, Tammuz, the 'Son of the Great Mother', was an historic king, said to have been crowned and reanimated by his mother. All the early kings were called sons of the Great Mother. They maintained with their own vigour the life and fertility of the country, and when they grew old they were supposed to have been put to death, although there are far more stories of the young men and women who were killed in place of the king than of the killing of the king himself.

The most important building of each Sumerian state was its temple, for the priesthood was immensely wealthy, owning a great many farms. These temples, though at first quite small, eventually comprised a number of buildings, including the living quarters of the priests, cells for pilgrims and storage rooms for the farm produce and the treasures of gold and other valuables.

Close by, though separated from it, was the temple tower or ziggurat, which was built in the form of a series of cubes of decreasing size, to form a flat-topped pyramid, a symbolic representation of a mountain and a reminder of the mountainous country of their origin. Near the top, approached by a series of outside ramps, was a small temple and an altar, and here the most sacred ceremony of the year took place, when each spring a young priest and priestess were led up to it to consummate a symbolic union, in the presence of an officiating priest, to ensure the success of the new season's crop, and were then killed and buried. The Tower of Babel was most probably one of these ziggurats.

The irrigated land of Mesopotamia was wonderfully fertile, and the Sumerians attained a high degree of material prosperity. From about 4300 B.C. they were using copper, lead and gold for various small ornaments, and they soon discovered the process of alloying copper with tin to produce bronze.

There are no native metals in the country and they established wide-ranging trade routes to acquire it, obtaining tin from eastern Iran, Asia Minor and Syria, gold from Elam, Cappadocia and Anatolia, silver and lead from the Taurus mountains and Elam, copper from Oman, the Persian Gulf and perhaps the Caucasus, building stone from Oman, lapis lazuli from Iran and Afghanistan, mother of pearl from the Persian Gulf, and cedar and pine from the mountains of the Lebanon and the Zagros mountains of Iran.

By 3500 B.C. they had invented the art of writing, which was first a series of pictograms, used as domestic records by the temple officials, but was soon reduced to simple hieroglyphs, which were incised with a stylus on tablets of wet clay, producing wedge-shaped or cuneiform impressions. Their priests had devised a calendar, had made astronomical and mathematical observations and invented the sexagesimal system of numeration. Having invented the potters wheel, they were using solid wheels (made from carved planks) on chariots and wagons before 3000 B.C.; they also manufactured glass.

By this time life amongst the city dwellers of Sumer was highly organised and prosperous, and with prosperity came war, for not only was the wealth of the cities a temptation to bands of pastoralists from the surrounding highlands and deserts, but there was also increasing rivalry amongst the city states themselves.

Sir Leonard Woolley's excavations of the Royal tombs at Ur show how complicated the Sumerian civilisation had become by

3500 B.C. The graves were built of brick and stone and were vaulted and arched. Along with the dead king were buried a host of his subjects, who had been given cups of poison in order that they might die with their royal master; they were his courtiers, his soldiers, with their copper armour and spears, musicians with their golden harps, many women and their attendants. In one grave alone seventy people had died with the king. His chariot was buried with him, together with the beasts that had drawn it, and wagon loads of valuable furniture, jewellery and weapons, as well as food and drink for his journey to the next world.

For the next two thousand years there was no dramatic advance in Sumerian civilisation, much of the creative genius of the earlier generations being dissipated in wars between the states, but by the third millennium B.C. the Mesopotamian civilisation had spread through western Asia. Syria and Palestine had become lands of City States and in the Nile valley the civilisation of Egypt was rising.

For many years archaeologists believed that the Egyptian civilisation was older than that of Mesopotamia and an entirely independent manifestation of the human spirit, but the Neolithic culture of Egypt, with its farming and domestication of animals, was not indigenous to the Nile valley and neither were the characteristic wheat and barley on which the civilisation was founded. Nevertheless, it arrived very early, and thereafter the civilisation of Egypt, in many ways, developed independently, much of it slowly diffusing, through the centuries, throughout not only Africa but the whole world.

As with the rivers of Mesopotamia, the civilisation of Egypt was made possible only by its great river. In the last sixteen hundred kilometres of its course, the Nile flows through the deserts of Nubia and Egypt, receiving no tributaries. Below Khartoum, the river cuts its way down the African plateau in a series of six great cataracts, the lowest being at Aswan, after which it enters the gentle slope of the Nile valley, nearly a thousand kilometres long but never more than twenty-two wide. For long stretches it is only about three kilometres wide, and at one point only two hundred and twenty metres across. The river is flanked by the limestone cliffs of the high desert, which at times tower steeply to five hundred metres above the plain. And a hundred and sixty kilometres from the sea, as it enters the

Mediterranean coastal plain below Cairo, the Nile fans out into the wide and fertile delta of Lower Egypt, with a span of two hundred and forty kilometres.

These were the Two Lands, Upper and Lower Egypt, and the Delta was always the richer and more populous—the region of Sais and Buto, and later of Alexandria—but much of this early civilisation has been lost and nearly all the archaeological treasures of Egypt's past glory come from the valley between Cairo and Aswan, where the sand and the dry heat have preserved so much.

The natural southern boundary of Egypt is the cataract at Aswan, and from here the land is desert as far as the Delta, hot by day and cool by night. Day after day, all the year through, the sun rises in a cloudless blue sky, pours down its heat unfailingly, and sets over the western edge of the high desert in a blaze of colour. At night, in the clear, clean desert air, the stars are brilliant and the moon sheds light almost as bright as day. Human life has been made possible in the valley solely because of the Nile. Every summer its upper reaches receive tropical rains, so that each June the waters of the Egyptian part of the river begin to rise. By August the Nile overflows its banks and floods the narrow valley, depositing rich, fertile silt. From the middle of October the waters quickly subside and by late November nothing is left but wet mud, ready for planting.

In Paleaolithic times, the Nile valley was a tropical jungle haunted by crocodiles and hippopotamuses. Flint implements of the same age as those of Upper Palaeolithic Europe—perhaps some twenty thousand years old—have been found on the hill slopes of the valley above the jungle region, and also in the Sahara; these implements were made and used by ancestral Negroes and Caucasians at a time when the dessication of the Sahara was only just beginning and there were still patches of grassy steppe, with enough game to support a small migrant population.

People who had learnt the arts of the New Stone Age from its centre in western Asia arrived in the Delta, and possibly also in Upper Egypt, by way of the Red Sea. The settlements of the Delta immigrants are found on either side of the Nile, as far south as Badari, above Assuit. These Badarian people were agriculturalists, growing wheat and barley, as well as various vegetables. They had domesticated goats, sheep and cattle and they possessed finely-made flint implements, comparable with the Solutrean of Europe, for harvesting their crop, and flint-tipped arrowheads for hunting. They made pottery by hand and also basketry, and they were beginning to hammer copper for small beads. Both men and women wore personal ornaments—girdles, necklaces, anklets, bracelets and ear-rings of shell and bone— and although they wore little or no clothing they had learnt to spin and weave wool and flax.

They buried their dead in a simple hole in the ground, in a crouched position, laid usually on the right side, with the head at the western end of the grave. The bodies were clothed in linen and the women given a profusion of ornaments, which included ivory combs carved with animal heads. They also buried their domestic animals with great care, wrapped in linen.

The dawn of Egyptian history is obscure and controversial, but we know that more tribes followed the Badarians into the Delta. Their gods had survived from the earliest forms—the totem animals who protected the hunters—and these tribes were ultimately ruled by queens who wore the royal insignia of the vulture head-dress.

After about 5500 B.C. the evidence becomes clearer, and this period marks the beginning of pre-dynastic Egyptian history, when succeeding waves of immigrants from the East arrived— the ancestors of the present-day Egyptians.

In the Delta a people whose royal house bore the insignia of the Cobra was established, but they were superseded by another Delta royal family, the Hornets. The crown was a high, red cap, rising at the back into a peak, and the badge of the country was the papyrus plant.

From about 5000 B.C. two kingdoms were established in Upper Egypt. To the north were the Reed people, whose king wore a high white, almost conical cap, and whose capital was not far from modern Cairo; to the south were the Hawks, whose country spread from about where Luxor now stands to the site of Edfu.

For close on two thousand years, these people were to live un-disturbed in the Nile valley, protected to east and west by the desert, to the north by the Mediterranean and to the south by the cataract at Aswan, beyond which lay 'the land of the spirits' and the Nubian desert.

They were too remote to be disturbed by invaders, yet near

enough to Mesopotamia to receive stimulus from the earlier civilisation and establish trade relations, and it was during these years that they evolved the civilisation on which that of dynastic Egypt was to be founded.

In the Nile valley they began to take advantage of the natural irrigation afforded by the annual Nile flood. They cleared the jungle and planted their crops in the residual mud. Land was precious, and they therefore buried their dead in the useless desert; in the burning hot, dry sand the bodies did not decompose, but quickly became dessicated and mummified.

They lived in small, totemic clans, their dwellings at first small reed huts on the edge of the desert above the valley. Their pottery was incised or painted with animal figures and they began to mine for their flint instead of using surface nodules. They also began to make stone vessels of alabaster and basalt, but it was not until comparatively late in pre-dynastic times, and at least a thousand years after metallurgy was being practised in western Asia, that they began an extensive use of metals, in addition to the earlier copper beads. Now they made copper axes, daggers and knives, obtaining the copper from the eastern desert and from Sinai, and in time they were acquiring supplies of lead and silver from Asia. They also began to manufacture faience, which is made from finely powdered quartz, fused and coated with glass.

Ornaments of lapis lazuli are found among their remains, and this stone was probably obtained from supplies which were, by this time, arriving regularly in Mesopotamia, from Afghanistan.

It was to be hundreds of years before Egypt had the wheel, but in pre-dynastic times they used asses for land transport and a primitive rowing boat made from bundles of reeds for river travel. Their dead were still buried in holes in the ground, but the structure of the graves was growing more complicated, with shelves for the increasing number of offerings.

The scattered villages developed into distinctive tribal districts. The old animal gods were still worshipped and each district or nome had its divine protector, but to these gods were now added the sun god Ra and also Osiris, the son of the earth god Seb and the sky goddess Nut. Osiris personified the yearly decay and revival of vegetation and like Adonis of later Greek times, he was thought to die and be reborn each year.

It was in the Delta that Egyptian civilisation first made its appearance, with the creation of the city state, the invention of writing, the use of metals and the creation of a fixed calendar, and there were organised states in the western Delta with a king, while the people in the valley were still living in their village communities of independent tribal units.

The Hawk King Meni was said to have unified all the nomes of Lower and Upper Egypt into a single realm and founded the first dynasty, but the process must have been a gradual one, involving a great deal of rethinking and pragmatism on the part of the kings and priests. Unlike Sumer, where the ruler was the deputy of the gods and not himself divine, in Egypt the ruler was himself the god incarnate, and to achieve this position a large literature of myths was created.

Egyptian tradition makes Osiris, the vegetation god and son of the Great Mother of the Asiatic religion, the first Egyptian king, and the pastoral staff and flail of Osiris were the insignia of the monarchs throughout the whole of Egyptian history.

Osiris maintained with his own vigour the life and fertility of the country. When the living god grew old he had, therefore, to be killed off, so that a younger and more vigorous heir could maintain the well-being of the kingdom. Yet Osiris was a stranger, opposed by the earlier established animal gods of Egypt and slain by his rival Set. Horus, the Falcon god of one of the Delta nomes, was identified with Osiris as his son, and he avenged his father's death by vanquishing Set. And after this legendary conquest by Horus, every king was regarded as the successor and divine embodiment of Horus. Osiris was now looked upon as a former king and always a dead king, who ruled over the land of the dead, while every living king was the embodiment of Horus: and it was his function and duty to maintain the cult of his dead father, for it was Osiris who conferred the benefits on the country.

Meni, traditional founder of the first dynasty of Egypt, came to the throne about 3407 B.C. He wore the red crown of the Hornet kings of Lower Egypt combined with the white crown of the Reed kings of Upper Egypt, and by marrying a wife descended from the ancient line of Vulture Queens he also became the Lord of the Vulture and the Cobra and was known as the Pharaoh.

Meni built the city of Memphis for his capital, at the head of the Delta, near where the Arab city of Cairo now stands, but

on the west bank of the Nile. The art of building in stone had
not yet begun, although craftsmen were already carving magnificent stone statues. Houses and public buildings were of white-
washed sun-dried brick, with wooden beams and pillars which
were carved and gaily painted. The floors were covered with
reed mats. Tables, chairs, couches and chests were carved and
beautifully inlaid with ebony and ivory. Vessels and trinket
boxes were of alabaster, crystal and blue glazed pottery, all
most delicately made. People were dressed in fine linen and wore
jewellery of turquoises, amethysts, carnelians and finely-wrought
gold.

There were thirty-three dynasties of Pharaohs before Egypt
was invaded by the Romans in 30 B.C., the periods having been
arbitrarily but conveniently defined by the Greek historian,
Manethro, and during this span of over three thousand years the
names of three hundred and fifty Pharaohs were recorded.

The line of succession was through the eldest daughter, but
the Pharaoh usually nominated a male heir, who more often
than not was his son, and to make the succession legal the new
Pharaoh married his sister, who became queen, though he was
also entitled to as many other wives as he wished.

The first eight dynasties of Egypt, covering a thousand years,
are known as the Old Kingdom, and it was during the second
dynasty that the first stone buildings began to appear. Egyptians
still knew nothing of the wheel, nor had they any horses, and it
was to be another three thousand years before the camel was
introduced into the country. The huge blocks of limestone and
granite were therefore transported by boat and sledge.

It was during this dynasty that the sun god Ra began to
assume an increasing importance in Egyptian religion, and at
Heliopolis, the City of the Sun, near Memphis, the small community of the priests of the sun god gradually extended their
power. Already they had acquired a reputation for great wisdom,
especially in astronomy, and they made their sacrifices to the sun
in the inner sanctuary of their temple, beside a sacred stone
which was fashioned in the form of a small pyramid.

They had a calendar, based on the rising of the star Sirius,
beginning their year on the day that the Nile floods began to
subside, so that their first season was that of the planting and
sowing time; and they had also devised a Nilometer for measuring the rise and fall of the flood waters.

The cult of Ra was at first confined to Heliopolis, where the interest in the sun was stimulated by the astronomical studies of the priests and their compilation of the calendar, and a solar theology was conceived. Ra was only a speculation and never a living king. He was pieced together from existing elements of thought. The priests of Heliopolis created the idea of a world in the sky where the Pharaoh could live eternally with the gods, and the sun being so dominant a feature of the Egyptian landscape, the idea was quickly accepted and Ra was included in the long list of the Pharaoh's names.

And it was in connexion with Ra that the earliest of the stories telling of the destruction of mankind arose, for it was said that his subjects became angry with him because, when he became old, he refused to sacrifice himself, according to the custom of the god-kings. Ra therefore persuaded his Mother goddess Hathor, to slay them. In her guise of Sekhmet, the lioness, she willingly set to, but having tasted blood, there was no stopping her, until the nervous subjects who still survived hit upon the brilliant idea of making her so drunk that she became incapable. Ra won his point. Henceforth, unlike Osiris, Ra was not killed when he grew old but was rejuvenated by the blood and sacrifice of his subjects.

By associating Ra with the Pharaoh, the Pharaoh gained tremendous power over his people. He no longer needed to be sacrificed in order to maintain the well-being of the kingdom. The blood of a few hundred lesser mortals was a fair substitute and these were usually slaves or prisoners of war, the motive for the war in the first place having probably been to acquire them for sacrifice.

The Heliopolitan priesthood aspired to supreme power amongst the priesthoods supporting the king, but the function of the Pharaoh was still based on the cult of Osiris, his dead father: and Ra, who had never been a king on earth, had no son.

By devious means, he had to become a father. This was achieved when a magician told King Khufu of the fourth dynasty that three children to be born of the wife of a certain priest of Ra were begotten by Ra himself, who had impersonated the Pharaoh and had intercourse with her. The fiction was embellished and made more confused by the secondary story that Ra had told Khnum, the potter god, to make two embryo children to place in the mother's womb, to be born in the usual way.

This story was so successful that it was obviously what a number of important people wanted to believe, and from this time the royal power passed into the hands of the Heliopolitan priesthood. Ra, the sun god, was the divine ruler of Egypt and the Pharaoh was now called the Son of the Sun, the physical son of a living deity, himself a semi-god and no longer the son of a dead king.

The Heliopolitans split the ruling group of Egypt into two parts, the ruling family connected with the sky and the sun god, who were buried in massive pyramid tombs, and the older ruling family and related nobility, who were connected with Osiris and went to the Other World by way of their mastaba tombs.

These developed from the simple graves of the earlier days. By late pre-dynastic times they had become large rectangular, brick-lined vaults, properly roofed with bricks or branches of trees, and they evolved into underground dwellings with suites of rooms, in which the ghost of the dead was supposed to live, while his physical existence continued in the underworld.

The Egyptians believed that immortality might be granted if they restored the vital elements missing in the dead body. The ritual of mummification began in the first dynasty, its aim being to preserve the body. Death masks and portrait statues were made, the creation of a statue being the same as rebirth. A statue-house and a chapel for offerings, where living friends could hold communication with the dead, were built in place of the single vaults and were the first mastaba tombs. It later came to be believed that the living could keep the dead alive in the next world, thereby securing for them immortality, by observing detailed funerary rites.

At first immortality was of the body rather than the spirit, so the dead had to be physically reborn as a prelude to immortality, but later the rituals were more concerned with the spiritual rebirth.

Osiris was the first king to die and be reborn to an immortality in some other world. Mummification was first confined to the kings, every king becoming Osiris and ruling over the dead, but at the same time he was living in his tomb, and his portrait statue could be animated by the libation of life-giving water, the burning of incense which gave him the odour of a living man, and the ceremony of opening the mouth. Though the portrait statue obviously remained inanimate, these rites satisfied the mourners that the statue was, in fact, alive.

There was a good deal of muddled thinking and self-delusion here, for the Egyptians of the Osiris cult believed that the dead were alive in the tomb and at the same time enjoying life in the land of the dead, which was at first underground and later in the Isles of the Blest, somewhere in the Nile delta.

With the Heliopolitan solar theology, the life in the hereafter was in the sky and proved a greater attraction. In time Osiris himself was elevated to the sky and became associated with Ra, and Horus, in the form of the divine falcon, became another manifestation of the sun god.

Zoser, the second king of the third dynasty, built the first pyramid for the reception of his body, about the year 2800 B.C. This was the step pyramid at Sakkara, near Memphis, which was composed of blocks of limestone in the form of truncated pyramids of diminishing size, which gave a stepped effect. It reached to a height of over sixty-five metres and was built over a deep vault lined with granite which had been quarried and floated down river from the first cataract.

In the paved courtyard surrounding the pyramid Zoser had a temple built, with magnificently carved portrait statues. The architect was Imhotep, his prime minister, a man whose wisdom and skill in medicine as well as architecture made him as venerated as the Pharaoh himself, so that after his death he also came to be regarded as a god, and centuries later was identified with the Greek god of medicine, Asklepios.

Snofru, the last king of the dynasty, was sending expeditions to Syria for timber from the cedar forests of Lebanon, to the Red Sea hills for gold, to Sinai for copper and malachite, and to the country of the Negroes, beyond the first cataract, to stop their attempted incursions into Egyptian territory.

Snofru's tomb was the first to be built in the form of a true pyramid, similar in shape to the sacred symbol in the sun priests' temple at Heliopolis, but it was during the fourth dynasty that the great pyramids of Gizeh were built, Khufu, the founder of the dynasty and the first Son of the Sun, building the stupendous Great Pyramid near Memphis, and within sight of Heliopolis, which was composed of 2,300,000 blocks of limestone, each weighing some two and a half tonnes, and surpassing in size and grandeur all those which were built by succeeding Pharaohs of the dynasty.

It seems likely that the Sphinx was also carved some time

during the fourth dynasty. It is a huge lion, which was a royal animal, with a male human head wearing a royal head-dress. It was carved from a natural formation of rock and it probably represents a manifestation of Ra.

The Old Kingdom lasted in Egypt for over a thousand years, during which time the Egyptians came to feel themselves a race apart, especially blessed by their sun god, so that not only the king but the nobles and the peasants were entitled to a life after death in Ra's heavenly kingdom.

Towards the end of the sixth dynasty came the first signs of the decline of monarchial power. For a time the governors of the nomes assumed increasing authority, thereby creating a land of independent feudal lords, similarly to that from which the first dynasty had been created. However, the tradition of kingship survived in Egypt with the creation, from the chaos of the eighth dynasty, of the ninth dynasty, established in 2271 B.C. by King Akhtoi and marking the beginning of the Middle Kingdom.

King Akhtoi developed into a grim tyrant and came to a bad end, for he was "seized with madness and devoured by a crocodile", but the third King Akhtoi of this dynasty, who reigned from 2252 to 2227 B.C., was a man of great wisdom. His letters to his son show his concern for the changing character of mankind. "Be diplomatic in speech ... speech is more powerful than any armament, none being able to circumvent a clever speaker," he wrote. "Respect a life of energy, for self-complacency will make a wretched man of you; yet a fool is he who is greedy of what others possess ... Take care that you do not punish wrongfully.

"Slay not any man that is about you, for God, in whose care he is, commends him to you ... Do not make any distinction between the son of a noble and one of humble birth; but take a man to you because of his merits ... Indolence would ruin heaven itself."

Akhtoi's son did not reign for long, dying without an heir, and there followed another period of confusion and anarchy in Egypt, at the end of which time a family of the southern kingdom became the royal house for the whole of the country, with Thebes, the modern Luxor, as capital. Karnak was the temple of the local Theban god, Amun, and it now became the most important centre of worship in the country, as Amun, rising in power and importance like his earthly manifestation, the new

Pharaoh, became the most important of the gods. To the fury of the priests of Heliopolis, he was identified with Ra and was known as Amun-Ra.

This dynasty of seven Pharaohs was the eleventh and it lasted for a hundred and sixty years, from 2271 B.C. to 2111 B.C. In Egypt it was a time of replanning and much building, but in Mesopotamia there was war.

The Sumerians had attained great wealth but with it had come an increasing rivalry between the city states, many of which now supported independent dynasties of rulers. The northern part of Mesopotamia, the land of Akkad, had come under the domination of Semitic dynasties, and about 2300 B.C. Sargon of Akkad marched south, conquered the whole of the country and united Sumer and Akkad under one strong rule. Sargon's conquests stretched from Elam to the cedar forests of Lebanon and the silver mountains of Taurus. He is even said to have "crossed the sea of the setting sun and caused the booty of the Sea Lands to have been brought over", which suggests that he reached as far as Cyprus.

Sargon's dynasty lasted for more than a hundred years, during which time his grandson conquered Magan and Elam and the mountains of Kurdistan and Armenia, but in Mesopotamia itself, the heart of the empire, this was a time of peace and increasing prosperity, with Semites and Sumerians absorbing the same culture and extending their foreign trade through the whole of the Near and Middle East, from Syria to India.

The Sargonid empire fell, however, with invasions of hill tribes from the north—'the habitation of the pest'—and during the anarchy which followed Mesopotamia became again a land of independent city states. For a brief spell of glory Ur, under its third dynasty, rose to great splendour, but by about 2025 B.C. Mesopotamia was attacked and conquered by the nomadic Amorites of the Arabian desert to the west and by Elamites from the east.

During these years the eleventh dynasty of Pharaohs in Egypt were building some of their finest tombs and temples. In the western desert, opposite Thebes, at the foot of the cliffs of the high desert, in a natural amphitheatre, now known as Deir-el-Bahri, Mentuhope II, fourth king of the dynasty, built a mausoleum with tombs for six of his wives and for himself a great pyramid tomb, with a wide courtyard and pillared arcades.

His successor, Amenemhet, founded the twelfth dynasty in 2111 B.C. and at the beginning of his reign, during a period of unusual drought throughout the whole of the Near East, a band of Semites arrived, driving their flocks and herds into the Delta for water and pasturage. Amenemhet ordered them to leave, for Egypt was also suffering from the drought, and among the tribesmen whom he deported was Abram, the patriarch of the nation of the Jews.

"And there was a famine in the land; and Abram went down into Egypt to soujourn there, for the famine was grievous in the land . . .

"And Pharaoh commanded his men concerning him, and they sent him away, and his wife, and all that he had. And Abram went up out of Egypt . . . up to the place where his tent had been at the beginning, between Beth-el and Hai . . ."

Throughout the following years there was more trouble for Egypt from the Negroes of the south. Sesuri III of the twelfth dynasty, who was Pharaoh from 1998 B.C. to 1959 B.C., invaded the Sudan. He re-established the Egyptian frontier at the second cataract and had an inscription carved on the boundary stone declaring that it had been set up "in order to forbid any Negro (except by special permission) to pass it by water or by land, either with a ship or with any herds of cattle, for ever".

During the next reign the swamps of the Fayum were reclaimed and drained to form a vast reservoir, fed by a canal dug parallel to the Nile. This is Joseph's canal, for Joseph, Abram's great-grandson, may well have helped in its construction during his year in Egypt, after Potiphar, the Egyptian, had bought him from the Israelites.

This was a period of great commercial activity in Egypt and one of the officers in charge of an expedition to the copper mines of Sinai recorded, rather smugly: "I treated my men with great kindness and I never shouted at the workmen."

The twelfth dynasty was a period of wonderful prosperity, during which Egyptian art and literature were at their best and the people at their most humanitarian, advocating kindness to the old and widowed and mercy to their enemies, but with the death of the great Amenemhet III there followed a period of confusion and misgovernment.

About 1860 B.C., when Pharaoh Neferhotpe was reigning in Upper Egypt, the eastern part of the Delta was invaded by Semitic tribes against whom the Egyptians of Lower Egypt were no match, for they came in horse-drawn, wheeled chariots. These were the Hyksos or 'Shepherds', racially a mixture of the Syrians and the ancestors of the Jews, dark, black-bearded men who came from Palestine and the eastern fringes of the Egyptian Delta.

Three years after the first invasion, the Hyksos had appointed their most important chief as king of the eastern Delta and he was accepted by the conquered Egyptians as their Pharaoh Sanati, the first of the Hyksos kings of the fifteenth dynasty.

For Egypt this was the beginning of total conquest, and by 1800 B.C. the Hyksos had gained control of the whole country and were ruling from Memphis, the Hyksos kings assuming all the ancient Egyptian titles and adding to them their own proud rank of Prince of the Desert.

For Egypt the old days of isolation were over and under the Hyksos commercial expeditions from Egypt ranged further afield, reaching as far as Mesopotamia in the east and Crete to the north, where the wonderful civilisation of the Minoans was beginning to flower. Large numbers of Israelites moved into Egypt at this time, and in Mesopotamia the Amorite Hammurabi, who reigned from 1800 B.C. to 1760 B.C. expelled the Elamites, conquered the whole of Mesopotamia and established the first dyasty of Babylon.

Hammurabi consolidated his empire, appointing governors for each of the city states. He drew up a code of laws and established a state religion based on the cult of Marduk.

About a hundred and fifty years after Hammurabi's death, the Hittites, who had grown in strength in the mountains of Anatolia, suddenly swooped down on to Mesopotamia. In 1895 B.C. they sacked the beautiful city of Babylon, but they withdrew before the invading Kassites of the east, who established a dynasty in Babylon which lasted until 1171 B.C., during which time the Assyrians of the north of the country emerged as a powerful state and a potential menace to the Babylonians.

From 1800 B.C. to 1600 B.C., while Hammurabi's Babylon was at the summit of its power and prestige, the Egyptians were putting up a fierce resistance to the Hyksos, and by 1576 B.C. the Thebans, helped by Negro warriors trained by Egyptians, succeeded in turning them out of the country, this date coinciding with the Biblical record of the beginning of the oppression of the

Israelites in Egypt, which was to continue for another two hundred and fifty years before their final expulsion.

The conquering Theban king who now became Pharaoh of Egypt was Ahmose and his accession marked the end of the Middle Kingdom, the beginning of the New Kingdom and the opening of the wonderful eighteenth dynasty.

Ahmose was succeeded by his son Amenhotep I, a man of great piety whose reign was peaceful, apart from a few campaigns against the Negroes of the Sudan and the tribesmen of the western desert.

He built a temple for the service of his spirit in the western desert opposite Thebes, the first of the group of temples known as Medinet Habu, but when it came to choosing a site for his tomb he found a hiding place which he hoped, though in vain, would be safe from tomb robbers, in a shallow ravine at the top of the western cliffs. He ordered a deep pit to be dug, with a flight of steps leading into a tunnel, at the end of which was the tomb chamber. After the interment of his body, the entrance was carefully sealed.

His successor, Thutmose I, became an imperialist, and after securing a new frontier in the Sudan, below the third cataract, turned eastwards from the Delta through Palestine and over the Lebanon to Aleppo, eventually reaching the Euphrates and laying claim to the whole of Syria, on which he imposed an annual tribute.

He devoted the rest of his reign to adorning Imperial Egypt with immense buildings suited to her new wealth and status, and for his tomb he chose a site near that of Amenhotep I, in what has now become known as the Valley of the Tombs of the Kings.

His daughter Hatshepsut succeeded him, first with her younger brother Thutmose II and, on his death, with her nephew Thutmose III, whom she largely disregarded, holding her separate court with a splendour which had never been surpassed in all the world. From her famous expedition to Punt, her emissaries brought back panther skins, ostrich feathers, ivory, ebony, antimony, gold, silver, living incense trees, and giraffes, panthers, baboons and monkeys.

Hatshepsut built for herself a great mortuary temple at Deir el Bahri, where the pyramid temple of Mentuhope of the eleventh dynasty already stood. Hatshepsut's temple had terraces of paved courtyards, in front of which were magnificent colonnades, and the limestone cliffs which towered behind it concealed the strange and desolate Valley of the Kings. Yet for all the ingenuity of the Pharaohs, that of the tomb robbers was greater, and it was not long before they discovered most of their hiding places and, defying the wrath of the gods, plundered them remorselessly.

When Hatshepsut died Thutmose III had himself recrowned Pharaoh and in 1471 B.C. set forth to consolidate the supremacy of Egypt over all the countries bordering the eastern Mediterranean. He waged one victorious campaign after another against the city states of Syria, and the rest of the world came to revere Egypt as the mother of a great empire.

Thutmose III conquered the King of Kadesh, whose city was built on the Orontes, a hundred miles from Damascus. He captured the city of Megiddo, on the western edge of the plain of Esdraelon. Each year he returned in triumph to his capital at Thebes, his army bearing vast hoards of treasure. From Megiddo alone his booty included a thousand chariots, more than two thousand horses, two thousand head of cattle, quantities of gold and silver, gorgeous armour and a royal tent.

The coffers of Egypt were full to overflowing with fabulous riches. Each conquered city state had to send its annual tribute to Thebes, and resident Egyptian governors in Syria saw to it that payment was regular and adequate.

The countries surrounding the empire, anxious to remain on friendly terms with mighty Egypt, also sent regular diplomatic gifts as tokens of goodwill, as well as entering into trade relationships. To the north of Syria was the kingdom of Mitanni, a useful buffer state between the Egyptian empire and the Hittites of Anatolia, and friendly messages and gifts came from here, as well as from the King of the Hittites, from Cyprus, from Knossos in Crete, from the islands of the Aegean and from the King of Babylon.

Thutmose III was a great general, whom his admirers described as "a circling comet which shoots out its flames and in fire gives forth its substance" and as a "lord of radiance, shining in the faces of his enemy". He was also a wise man, and amongst the many pieces of advice he gave to his prime minister, he said: "The position of Prime Minister is not sweet; it is bitter; and you must see that you do everything according to law and according to the right, for it is an abominable thing to show partiality..."

Do not be angry with a man unjustly, for the proper dread of princes is in their doing justice."

The successors of Thutmose III were Amenhotep II and Thutmose IV, who ably maintained the prestige of the empire. Then came Amenhotep III and his son Amenhotep IV, the most interesting of all the eighteenth dynasty Pharaohs, who married Nefertiti and who later changed his name to Akhnaton. He reigned from 1375 B.C. to 1358 B.C. and has been called the "first individual in human history".

When he ascended the throne of Egypt the pace of civilisation was quickening throughout Asia, and reaching into Europe.

CHAPTER EIGHT

Civilisations of the Indus, China, Crete and the Middle East

By the third millennium B.C. there were farming communities in the north-west of Pakistan which had trade contacts through the Persian Gulf with Mesopotamia, and by about 2500 B.C. a civilisation had developed in the Indus valley which had been inspired by the achievements of Sumer—although, in detail, it was to develop independently, through the creative genius of the indigenous inhabitants.

This early Indus civilisation came a thousand years after the beginning of the Sumerian civilisation, and some five hundred years after that of Egypt.

The two best known sites are those of Mohenjo-dara and Harappa, capital cities of a crescent of land stretching for sixteen hundred kilometres from the coast of the Arabian Sea to the hills of Simla, at a time when the great Sind plain was well-watered compared with the arid conditions of today.

It was a civilisation of scattered small towns and trading centres, and of the two main centres Harappa was built on the banks of the Ravi river, in the Punjab, and Mohenjo-daro, of which far more has survived, nearly six hundred and fifty kilometres to the south-west, on the main Indus river.

The Indus civilisation was based on the agriculture of the fertile valley, where they grew wheat and barley, vegetables and fruit, as well as the earliest cotton in the world. Their domesticated animals were cattle, camels, buffaloes, asses and horses. They evolved a form of elementary pictographic writing, which was stamped on seals, scratched on pottery and inscribed on copper tablets, but it has not yet been deciphered. They had specialised craftsmen who were maintained by the surplus food grown by the surrounding farmers, the crafts including metallurgy, wheel-made pottery, faience, gem-cutting and ship-building for their overseas trade with Mesopotamia, by way of the Persian Gulf and Bahrain.

Those who were not engaged in agriculture lived in well-planned cities and exercised political sway over large areas of the surrounding countryside. Mohenjo-daro was about one and a half kilometres square and divided by wide main streets crossing each other at precise right-angles, thus separating the city into blocks of about four hundred metres by two hundred and forty metres. Within each block was a network of small alleys giving access to close-set, flat-roofed, box-like little houses, built mostly of mud brick and timber. The plan was extraordinarily rigid and symmetrical, utterly unlike the labyrinths of narrow lanes with hovels set all hugger-mugger in unexpected corners, which were to arise in later cities of the East.

The houses of the wealthy, built of baked brick, were more spacious, with blank walls to the street and all the rooms facing inwards on to an interior courtyard.

The streets were unpaved, but beneath them were built arched brick sewers with manholes into which the drains from each house emptied. Houses were also provided with rubbish chutes which emptied into brick street bins, amenities which, with the excellently maintained wells, were far in advance of anything that either the Indus valley or the rest of the world was to see again for thousands of years.

It was an ordered and peaceful society, and there are no indications that they were ruled by kings or a military caste. In each city was a large citadel, in part of which was the grain store. At Mohenjo-daro was a range of buildings which may have been the homes of a priest and a colony of monks, suggesting that the civilisation was a theocracy, governed by the priests. Here the most interesting feature of the citadel is the large bath, which perhaps inaugurated the cleansing practices of the Hindus.

The religion of the Indus valley people was based on the Old World cult of the Mother Goddess and many terra cotta figurines of her have come to light, but also stone amulets have been found suggesting phallus worship and half-human half-animal figures, the beginning of a cult from which the worship of Siva, the Lord of the Beasts, was to evolve.

The civilisation lasted for nearly a thousand years, and then suddenly collapsed. Towards the end it may have been declining because of the decreasing rainfall, but from the broken skulls and scattered bones found in the streets of Mohenjo-daro, the end was violent and terrible. They were overwhelmed by an invasion of Aryans—Indo-European barbarians and cattle thieves, who came in horse-drawn chariots, slaughtered the people of Mohenjo-daro and left their bodies unburied where they fell.

It was these invaders who settled in the country and founded the historic dynasties of India, but the indigenous population survived, probably as slaves, still worshipping their ancient gods, which in time took their place in the Indian pantheon.

There were Neolithic settlements in the sparsely populated basin of the Yellow river of north China from about 2500 B.C. to 2100 B.C., growing millet, wheat and probably rice. They had domesticated animals which included pigs, cattle, sheep, dogs and possibly horses, and also chickens. They made pottery by hand and wove silk from the silk worm which, in addition to a coarse, woven hemp cloth, was used for clothing.

The knowledge of agriculture and the domestication of animals had infiltrated to north China from the centres of the Old World civilisation by way of Iran and the Oxus river, Samarkand and Kashgar, Sinkiang and the Gobi desert, the route which was later to become the 'silk road' followed by the Greeks and after them by the medieval travellers, including Marco Polo.

From 2100 B.C. the first civilisation—the Shang Dynasty—was established in the Yellow river basin, probably inspired by travellers from the west, for it followed the pattern of the earlier civilisations, although it was to develop independently and, being so remote, it borrowed even fewer elements from Mesopotamia than the Indus valley civilisation.

By about 1500 B.C. the royal capital city of the Shang dynasty had been built at An-yang, with a society that resembled in many ways that of the Near East Bronze Age people. The king, in his pillared palace, was deified after death, and human beings, most of them slaves or prisoners of war, were sacrificed at his funeral.

There were two classes, the warrior nobility, serving the king, and the peasants and artisans, many of whom were superb craftsmen, particularly in bronze-working. They made eating and drinking vessels, cooking pots, tools and weapons of bronze, and the sacrificial bronze vessels in which they offered their sacrifices to the gods and the ancestors were richly ornamented with patterns in low relief, masterpieces of bronze casting by the cire perdue method, which very early assumed the characteristic Chinese forms, such as the three-footed bowl.

They had chariots with spoked wheels drawn by a pair of horses, which were remarkably like those of the Mycenean princes, and the chariots and horse fittings were all of bronze.

Their foreign trade though not large was far-reaching, links having been traced as far west as the Black Sea, where it met the eastern trade of Mycenae, while to the north they ranged into Finland and Sweden—yet in style all their art forms, their beautiful jade and ivory carvings, their inlaid work in wood and bone, their lacquer and their gold ornaments remained distinctively Chinese.

They devised the form of writing from which modern Chinese characters have developed and examples have survived on thousands of 'oracle' bones. These were small pieces of stone or tortoise shell on which they inscribed questions to the gods, the answers being interpreted by the shapes of the cracks which developed after the oracle bones had been submitted to fierce heat.

The Shang dynasty lasted for about a thousand years and was then overthrown by a less highly developed people, the Chous, who emerged from the mountains of Shensi and captured the capital about 1030 B.C. But the Chous absorbed the Shang civilisation and not only preserved the continuity but also extended the borders of their state north to Manchuria and south to the Hwai valley, where people were still living in a Neolithic culture, to bring them under the influence of civilisation.

The Chou dynasty lasted for the next five hundred years or so, and during this time, about 500 B.C., Confucious was born and the traditions and manners of the Chinese were formulated, inspired perhaps by the belief that the world had once known a happier existence. Kwang-Tze, a follower of Lao-Tze, who lived from 604 B.C. to 532 B.C., wrote of his master and the Taoist religion: "In the age of perfect virtues, men attached no value to wisdom. They were upright and correct, without knowing that to be so was Righteousness: they loved one another, without knowing that to do so was Benevolence: they were honest and leal-hearted, without knowing that it was Loyalty; they fulfilled their engagements without knowing that to do so was Good Faith."

After Fu-hi and other sovereigns disturbed the harmonies of heaven and earth, said Kwang-Tze, "the manners of the people, from being good and simple, became bad and mean".

This was a fair comment on the degradation of the human spirit and the melancholy sequence of avarice and violence which came with all civilisations.

After the Chou dynasty came the brief power of the Ch'ins, an intrusive tribe from the border country who built the Great Wall and extended the empire southwards to the Canton delta. They were followed by the Han dynasty which lasted from about 202 B.C. to A.D. 220 and during this time the heart of the empire shifted to the basin of the Yangtse river and the silk trade was established with the Roman Empire.

The first European civilisation was on the island of Crete, which had been first inhabited and colonised by Neolithic people from Asia Minor, although from 3000 B.C. the Cretans had been greatly influenced by Egypt, from whom they had learnt the arts of pottery and copper working, and with whom they carried on a peaceful trade. They were essentially a maritime people who grew wealthy from sea trade with Egypt and the countries of the eastern Mediterranean. Their civilisation has been called Minoan, after the legendary King Minos, king and lawgiver of the island. who every eight years would retire alone to Mount Ida, the highest mountain in Crete, to render an account of his kingship to his heavenly father Zeus and receive guidance and renewed power for the years to come.

If he ever existed at all he must have arrived late in the period of Cretan civilisation, for he probably came from the mainland of Greece, The legend says that in revenge for the murder of his son by King Aegeus of Athens, which was then an insignificant little town, perhaps subject to Minos, the Athenians were bound to send to Crete every eight years seven youths and seven virgins. Their fate was to be incarcerated in the vast Labyrinth built by Daedalus, an Athenian exile, and sacrificed to the fierce Minotaur who lived there, a creature half bull, half human, whose existence replenished the life of the king and of the sun, of which he was the embodiment. Theseus, the son of Aegeus, volunteered to be one of the sacrificial victims and he and his companions set sail from Athens in a black-sailed boat, but when they arrived in Crete Ariadne, the daughter of Minos, fell in love with Theseus and helped him by drugging the guard of the Labyrinth, giving him a ball of thread by which he was able to trace his way through its perplexing complications, and a sword with which to slay the Minotaur. All went as planned and Theseus and his friends escaped back to Athens, but as they approached the Greek coast they forgot to hoist the white sail of victory and his father, seeing the black sail of mourning and thinking his son was dead, threw himself into the sea, which ever afterwards was called the Aegean.

The civilisation of Crete followed the pattern of the earlier civilisations of Mesopotamia and Egypt, beginning with an extensive use of copper for daggers and axes and collective megalithic tombs for successive generations of the dead. By the Middle Minoan period of about 2000 B.C. to 1580 B.C. there was a division of labour, with an advance in metallurgy and wheel-made pottery, and people had begun to live in towns, with rulers who had affinities with the gods and dwelt in palaces. They had wheeled transport and roads and from the keeping of accounts developed a written script—Linear A—which was inscribed on clay tablets and seals.

The palace of Knossos, which Sir Arthur Evans began to unearth in A.D. 1900 from a huge, unpromising mound, bare save for a few olive trees, proved to be a vast complex of build-ings covering nearly two and a half hectares and equipped with a remarkable system of drains and wells.

The archaeological evidence showed that the place had been destroyed by earthquakes and rebuilt several times, but the final, white-walled, pillared palace was a place of astonishing beauty. Although the Cretans had assimilated so much from Egypt, their art emerged as highly individual and the palace frescoes were ablaze with colour and a joyous, naturalistic representation of dancing girls and youths, of animals and birds, plants and flowers—reeds, lilies and seaweed—in a gay profusion.

There are many representations of the king in his feathered head-dress and of the bull. They worshipped the Earth Mother and the vaulting game is depicted, in which youths, with courage and agility, vaulted over the bulls, thereby presumably paying tribute to her by showing their faith in her power to protect them.

Many female figurines, probably of the Earth Mother, have been found at Knossos, all dressed in the Cretan costume of a high-waisted, long, full skirt, which gives them an oddly Edwardian look.

Every aspect of Minoan art, the delicately carved ivory, the bronze and gold work and the beautifully fine, painted pottery, was of rare beauty and the people seem to have been freer and less priest-ridden than their contemporaries on the mainlands.

About 1450 B.C. there was an assault on Knossos which was accompanied by a change in dynasty. This was probably an invasion from Greece, for the new rulers, amongst whom may well have been King Minos of the legend, introduced a new script—Linear B—which was in ancient Greek and in use on the mainland of Greece. But only fifty years later, in 1400 B.C., Crete was invaded by the Myceneans, a warlike people who had invaded Greece from Asia Minor and southern Russia many years earlier, and now emerged as the most dominant people of the Greek mainland.

The Myceneans sacked the palace of Knossos and it was never rebuilt, but in the course of establishing their own great civilisation, the first on the mainland of Europe, and their sea-carrying trade, they adopted and preserved much of Cretan culture.

This was the world into which Amenhotep IV of the eighteenth dynasty of Egypt was born, Pharaoh of the great Egyptian empire, for he came to the throne in 1375 B.C., shortly after the Myceneans had destroyed Knossos.

His marriage to Nefertiti, the daughter of Ay, an Egyptian nobleman, broke the tradition of marrying the Pharaoh to his eldest sister. Other wives were allotted to Akhnaton, amongst them a princess of Mitanni, but there are no records of his ever having lived with them. It was Nefertiti whom he loved and to whom he addressed his love poems, and he was to declare himself a monogamist.

Never before had there been such luxury as existed in the Nile valley during the early years of his reign. The houses of the great, gay with dancing girls and musicians, were decorated, like the palaces, with wonderful murals. The nobles and princes drank from cups of gold, silver and crystal. They held hunting parties and water festivals and at their sumptuous banquets they were attended by dozens of negro slaves. They dressed in fine linen embroidered with gold thread. They wore jewellery wrought with the most marvellous delicacy. Necklaces, bracelets, ear-rings, and circlets were of gold inlaid with turquoise, amethysts, carnelians, corals and garnets. Their chariots were gilded and the horses decked with ostrich plumes. The Pharaoh and his Queen were borne in gold carrying-chairs, their attendants running alongside, to fan them with ostrich plumes.

The peasants had declined in social status as the civilisation they supported created a king and a ruling class to order their lives. From Neolithic independence they had sunk to a state of docile acceptance of the economic and political plans of their masters. Materially they probably benefited from them, but since they were excluded from the literate and educated privileged classes, they sank into a state of sterile, unchanging conservatism.

They lived in their straw shelters or mud brick huts and ploughed with their wheel-less ploughs, much as they did until the present century. They hauled water from the Nile by means of the ancient, creaking *shaduf*, a method which was still being used in the 1940s. They made bricks with mud and straw, poured into moulds and left to dry in the sun. They sailed their feluccas, with their slender, triangular sails. The hieroglyph for a man shows him with a stick across his shoulders, his arms raised to support it at either end, and to this day Egyptian peasants stroll comfortably through the fields like this.

During the three months of the inundation, they were not able to work in the fields, and it was during this time that thousands of men helped with the gargantuan task of cutting and transporting the huge blocks of limestone and granite which were used in the building of the temples and monuments, although the highly skilled artisans worked at their trades all the year round.

Mining in the copper and gold mines was a hazardous business, for although there were still many open workings, there were already some quite deep and extremely narrow shafts in which the miners broke away the mineral-bearing rocks with wedges and hammers. The pits were lit by faggots of burning wood, soaked in resin and stuck to the walls with lumps of clay. With no ventilation and no precautions against flooding, accidents must have been frequent and fatal, but labour was abundant and cheap and the span of life, even for the highest in the land, was brief.

For the most part, the peasants seem to have prospered with the rising fortunes of the country, and the harbours of the Delta were busy with shipping laden with treasure from Cyprus, Crete and the isles of the Aegean, from Tyre and Sidon, Beirut and Byblos. At the quays along the waterfront at Thebes it arrived in a never-ending stream—gold dishes and drinking cups, vases of silver and lapis lazuli, daggers and swords, rare scented woods, faience and glass, horses, sheep and cattle, while from Nubia came ivory and gold, ostrich feathers, leopard skins and incense for the temples and palaces.

This vast treasure went first to the priests of Amun-Ra at the holy city of temples at Karnak, where the High Priest of Karnak divided it between the temple and the Pharaoh.

The priests of Amun-Ra were by now nearly as rich as the Pharaoh himself, yet they were growing uneasy, for the royal family and their court were showing an increasing interest in a new god from Syria. Ra was the god living in the sun, but this new religion was subtler, centring round Ra-Horakhti or Aton, the intangible power in the sun itself, by means of which Ra's existence was made possible.

Egypt's new position in the world, as an imperial power, affected her thinking. The Pharaoh was now receiving tribute from all the known world. He must, therefore, be the incarnation of a world god, a being greater than the purely Egyptian Amun-Ra, a god of the Empire, which all the peoples of the Empire, with their divers languages, nationalities, cultures and gods, would know and understand and worship. They chose Aton.

Amenhotep IV, who succeeded to the throne at the age of fourteen, became increasingly interested in Aton. He studied the complicated theology of Egypt, reflecting on his own titles—the Mighty Bull, Lofty of Plumes, King of Upper and Lower Egypt, Son of the Sun, Divine Ruler of Thebes, Beloved of Amun-Ra, and decided that he believed none of it.

At Karnak he saw the priests extracting penances from people who could ill afford to pay for them. In the crowded courts and precincts he saw the pedlars selling charms and amulets, pro-phylactics, aphrodisiacs, curses and pieces of good luck. The moral teaching of the temple was sound enough, but the whole organisation was corrupt, and to the young Pharaoh the priests seemed avaricious humbugs, battening on the credulity of the people by inducing them to placate and outwit the gods with expensive magical ritual.

He refused to acknowledge that he was the earthly manifesta-tion of Amun-Ra, declaring himself to be the chosen of Aton,

103

and he changed his name to Akhnaton. The High Priest of Karnak was deprived of his political post of Grand Vizier and thereby lost control of the foreign tribute. When he refused to allow Karnak to be rededicated to Aton, Akhnaton, with the support of Nefertiti, moved the court from Thebes, so that it was no longer the capital of Egypt, and built a new capital for himself on virgin soil, three hundred and twenty kilometres to the north, near Tel-el-Amarna.

The priests of Karnak were dispossessed. Though they still had immense accumulated wealth, they no longer received their share of the Empire's tribute. The trade and commerce of Thebes dwindled and the merchants and artisans fell on hard times, but at Amarna, the City of the Horizon, life, for a few halcyon years, was idyllic. Tribute arrived regularly. The princes of the Empire were loyal, and the caravan routes made safe from robbers.

Akhnaton pondered on the nature of Aton and gradually came to think of him as less tangible and more spiritual than the original Syrian conception. For Akhnaton, Aton became the power which created and motivated all forms of life. He was the Great Creator, the ultimate spirit of love and truth, the power that gave to life its happiness.

The symbol of Aton was the sun's disc, from which arms stretched protectively down to earth, but as Aton was a spirit no image was ever made of him and no human or animal sacrifices offered. Only flowers and fruit were brought to the temple. Fifteen hundred years before Christ was born, Akhnaton conceived a god like the God of Christianity, a God of truth, compassionate, merciful and tender, a God of peace, who would not tolerate violence and strife and hated deception and hypocrisy.

Akhnaton was also a poet. He wrote passionate love poems for Nefertiti, gentle little pieces for his small daughters, and hymns to Aton, which are reminiscent of the Psalms of David, written more than three hundred years later. "Thy love is great and large ... Thou fillest the two lands of Egypt with thy love ... Thy rays encompass the land ... Thou bindest them with Thy love ... All flowers blow and that which grows on the soil thrives at Thy dawning, O Aton ... All cattle leap upon their feet; the birds that were in the nest fly forth with joy; their wings which were closed move quickly with praise to the living Aton."

Passionately convinced that he had received a divine revelation, Akhnaton sent his missionary priests throughout Egypt to preach his new-found truth, but to people steeped in the traditions of material gods and sacrifices it was mostly incomprehensible.

Living in the palace was Smenkhkara, who seems to have been Akhnaton's half-brother and was given his eldest daughter, Merytaton, for a bride. Also at the court was a young prince Tutankhaton, whose parentage is not known, who was married to Akhnaton's third daughter, Enkhsenpeaton.

In Thebes conditions were growing desperate, and the rift between Karnak and Amarna deepened. When, after the funeral of Akhnaton's mother, Queen Tiy, the priests of Thebes re-dedicated her soul to the care of Amun, Akhnaton ordered the stonemasons to obliterate the name of Amun from every temple in the country, and forbade the worship not only of Amun but also of all the minor gods in the country. Henceforth Egypt was to be monotheistic.

Now came the first hint of trouble in the Empire. The Hittites were making raids into the kingdom of Mitanni. The King of Mitanni was murdered and his son allied himself with the Hittites in order to retain the throne. The King of Babylon complained that one of his caravans had been robbed while passing through Syria and demanded compensation. The Prince of Kadesh re-volted and declared Kadesh an independent kingdom again. He joined forces with the Hittites and began a full-scale invasion of Syria. King Aziru of the Amorites turned traitor, which meant that Simyra and Byblos were in danger.

All these messages—the Amarna letters—were in the form of cuneiform inscriptions on clay tablets, the diplomatic form of communication, and many have survived.

Akhnaton's counsellors begged him to send an army into Syria to check the Hittites and protect the remaining loyal princes of the Empire, but supported by Nefertiti, he refused to countenance any act of war or violence. For Akhnaton the means could never justify the end and he remained fanatically true to the tenets of his Aton religion.

Heartrending pleas for help came from the beleaguered cities as the Hittites, the cruellest enemies the world had ever known, steadily advanced, burning, pillaging and murdering on the way. From Tunip came the desperate message: "And now Tunip, your city, weeps, and her tears are running and there is no help for us."

The King of Sidon opened his gates to the perfidious Aziru.

Together they marched on Tyre. Megiddo and Askelon pleaded for help. From Jerusalem came a bitter cry: "The King's whole land will be lost. Everybody is ruined. . . ." Simyra was burnt to the ground. Byblos was surrounded.

At last Akhnaton yielded to the entreaties of his generals and agreed to send an army to save Byblos. Nefertiti left him, taking the daughters and also Tutankhaton, who was still only eight or nine years old, to her private palace at Amarna. The cause of the quarrel is not known. Could it have been because he had broken faith with their principle of pacifism?

Akhnaton, ill and distracted, now shared the throne with Smenkhara, bestowing on him the title of the beloved of Akhnaton. And knowing that he was dying, he appointed Smenkhara his successor, with Merytaton as Queen.

The relieving force arrived too late to save Byblos. It fell and then Beirut was lost.

These disasters followed each other over a period of some four years, during which the tribute grew steadily less and the coffers of Amarna relentlessly emptied. All was lost—the Lebanon, Askelon, Tyre and Sidon, Simyra and Byblos, Beirut, Jerusalem, Kadesh, Tunip and Aleppo, the Orontes valley and the Jordan: and refugees poured into Egypt, bitter and angry at their desertion by the mother country. Their people were starving. They were living "like the goats of the mountains", they cried.

Akhnaton, broken in spirit and health, was deemed unfit to be Pharaoh. Ay, Nefertiti's father, and Horemheb, commander-in-chief of the army, ordered Smenkhara and Merytaton back to the palace at Thebes, where they were commanded to restore the power of the Amun priesthood at Karnak, but for the next few weeks Smenkhara prevaricated.

As Akhnaton lay dying, Nefertiti returned to him, but when he died Smenkhara and Merytaton were secretly murdered and Tutankhaton, still only ten years old, was taken from Nefertiti's care, rededicated to Amun and renamed Tutankhamun. With his child wife he was hurriedly brought back to Thebes and the priests of Thebes, still rich with their hidden hoards of wealth, were supreme once more. The old gods, the old ways, the twilight of mysteries and oracles, terrors and superstitions, were back again, and Akhnaton's brief idyll of a heaven upon earth was over and finished for ever.

The beautiful city of Amarna was systematically destroyed.

Queen Nefertiti and her remaining four daughters were never heard of again and their graves have never been found.

Akhnaton was buried with his mother Queen Tiy in the Valley of the Tombs of the Kings, after being disinterred from his chosen burial place in the City of the Horizon, but a year or two later the Queen's coffin was moved and placed by the side of her husband's, Amenhotep III, and Akhnaton was left alone, in dishonour and ignominy. His name was blotted from the paintings in his shrine and cut from the gold ribbons which bound his body. By being made nameless, be became an outcast, condemned to eternal banishment, beyond the reach of all prayers and sacrifices, doomed to live for ever in the underworld, hungry, homeless, unloved and without hope of redemption.

Tutankhamun died when he was only nineteen, and Ay who succeeded him was an old man and ruled for only three or four years. The last Pharaoh of the dynasty was General Horemheb, who reigned from 1341 B.C. to 1317 B.C. He removed the last vestiges of Aton worship, glorified Karnak and the priests of Amun-Ra and, before he died, succeeded in reconquering part of the lost Egyptian empire in Syria.

The throne passed to his prime minister, Rameses I, who founded the nineteenth dynasty. This was still a time of great luxury and prosperity in Egypt. The horizon was broader and the nation more international in its outlook, by now employing both Negro and Asiatic slaves.

Rameses I's son, Sety I, led an army into Syria and reached as far as the Lebanon, but here he was checked by the growing might of the Hittites. His son Rameses II, also made a military expedition into Syria against the Hittites, with an army which contained a large proportion of foreign mercenaries from Syria and other Mediterranean countries, including Sardinia, Sicily, Greece and Crete.

All these campaigns were celebrated with new temple buildings and endowments to the priesthood of Amun-Ra, so that by the time of the accession of Rameses III, in 1174 B.C. it owned more than two hundred thousand hectares of land and a hundred thousand slaves, as well as entire cities in Syria and Nubia, with which the priests maintained contact with their own fleet of galleys.

At last, on the death of the last Rameses of the twentieth dynasty, in 1101 B.C., Heri-Hor, the High Priest of Amun, assumed the title of Pharaoh himself and Egypt became a theo-cracy, ruled by the priesthood of Karnak, and the religion of Amun-Ra, as expounded by the priests, was the law of the land.

It marked the end of Egypt's imperial and military strength, for when she was next invaded her powers of resistance had crumbled. And none of the civilisations of the Near East and western Asia had many more years to run.

During the twelfth century B.C. the Assyrians had emerged as a small but powerful state, with their capital city of Nineveh. During the seventh century B.C. they had, under Sennacherib, marched against the Elamites and then sacked Babylon. Here Sennacherib was murdered by his sons, but they were forced into exile when Prince Esarhaddon seized the throne and then sacked Sidon and invaded Lower Egypt. His son continued the march of terror, his army reaching up the Nile valley to sack sacred Thebes in 663 B.C.

A few years later they turned again on Elam, destroying all the cities and leaving Susa, the capital, in flames.

Yet by 612 B.C. the days of Assyrian empire were over. Nineveh was attacked by the nomadic Medes and Chaldeans and great Assyria had fallen. The Medes withdrew but the Chaldeans now ruled the former Assyrian Empire from Babylon, their king from 605 B.C. to 562 B.C. being Nebuchadnezzar, who attacked Judah and captured Jerusalem in 586 B.C., forcing the Jews into exile in Babylon.

While Nebuchadnezzar reigned in Babylon, the Persians, a race of peasants living in the mountains north of the Persian Gulf, as vassals of the Medes, gathered strength until they were able to establish a joint rule of Medes and Persians. In 540 B.C., under their leader Cyrus, the Persians marched against Lydia, the rich trading centre in western Asia Minor, whose king was Croesus. The armies met outside Sardis, the capital of Lydia, and victory went to Cyrus, who next turned on Babylon, which he captured about 539 B.C.

His son Cambyses extended the Persian Empire by attacking Egypt. It took only one battle to defeat the Egyptians. Cambyses marched through the Delta and seized Memphis. The Pharaoh was put to death and Cambyses crowned in his place, the first king of the twenty-seventh dynasty. He tried to extend his rule to include Cyrene and Carthage, which had been founded by the Phoenicians in 813 B.C., but this proved a costly failure, for most of his army perished in the desert. Then he turned south along the Nile valley, but again he met disaster, his men dying in their hundreds of sickness, thirst and starvation. Cambyses himself was driven near to insanity with his sufferings—pillaging and murdering, destroying the sacred shrines of Egypt and treating the priesthood with contempt.

It was his successor Darius who organised the vast Persian Empire. In Egypt he restored the priesthood and rebuilt many of the temples, and he was also responsible for the cutting of the first canal between the Mediterranean and the Red Sea, although it did not remain navigable for long.

At its zenith, the Persian Empire stretched from the Oxus and the Indus rivers in the east to Egypt in the west. Darius attempted to attack the Scythians—nomads of the plains of southern Russia bordering the Black Sea—by crossing the Hellespont on a bridge of boats and then the river Danube, but the Scythians eluded him, retreating all the time into the vast empty stretches of grassland, until Darius, outrunning his supply columns, was forced to give up the chase.

He made another attempt to enter Europe by attacking the Greeks, but in 490 B.C. his army was repulsed by the Greeks on the plains of Marathon. Ten years later Greek sailors sank the Persian fleet at Salamis. By 334 B.C. Alexander had set forth from Macedonia on his astonishing series of victories from Asia Minor to Iran and the Punjab which brought about the end of the Persian Empire.

The ancient civilisations of Mesopotamia and Egypt never recovered, and it was in Europe that the future development of world civilisation was to take shape.

CHAPTER NINE

The Bronze Age in Britain

By the sixteenth century B.C. there were dozens of small, independent communities in Greece and Asia Minor which had reached a high level of Bronze Age civilisation and grown prosperous with a trade in metals, and Mycenae became the most powerful of them all. Here, from the shaft graves in which, between about 1600 B.C. and 1450 B.C. the wealthy were buried, the treasure of gold and silver vessels, the bronze mirrors with carved ivory handles, the jewellery and beautiful weapons are evidence of the riches they had accumulated through their overseas trade and the export of their metal work and pottery, their flagons of wine and jars of oil.

At the height of their power, after the fall of Crete, they built the massive stone walls surrounding the five hectares of Mycenae and the Lion Gateway through which their 'god-born' king and the princes rode forth in their chariots, which so closely resembled those of the Hyksos and the Hittites. And for their kings they built huge circular, underground graves approached by a sloping passage and surmounted by a conical dome, sometimes, as in the vast grave of Agamemnon, soaring up to fifteen metres, the commoners being buried in rock-cut chamber tombs which served as family vaults for succeeding generations.

The Myceneans traded extensively with the walled city of Troy, which by this time had been rebuilt for the fifth time, with other cities of Asia Minor, and with Syria, Palestine, Egypt, Mesopotamia and the islands of the Mediterranean.

Although there was a fair supply of copper in the Mediterranean there was very little tin, and it was the demand for metals

110

—and also for the Baltic amber, with its magical 'electrical' properties—which opened up the trade routes through Europe and introduced metal working to the west.

However, before the full Bronze Age developed in Europe, the continent was subjected to a series of migrations of peoples from west to east and south to north, some peaceful, some warlike. During these incursions, which were probably due to a steadily increasing population seeking land space, many of the Neolithic peasants were submerged and new peoples of mixed and complicated blood came into existence.

The first important migration was from inland Spain, where people with a tradition of megalithic building began to move northwards and eastwards into central Europe, driven from their homeland by stronger people from the coast, perhaps, though this can be only surmise. Because of their characteristic bell-shaped pottery beakers, they are known as the Beaker people.

One branch moved into Brittany and the Channel Islands, but the larger and more important group migrated north-eastwards where, in the region of the Rhineland, they met another, more warlike group of people on the move, the Nordic Battle Axe people, who, by means of their characteristic heavy stone-axes, had established themselves through large areas of Europe, from the Baltic to the Black Sea.

These warrior people were a new kind of society which had arisen with the spread of civilisation—a hunting people who had acquired, by fair means or foul, the flocks and herds of the settled farmers and had become nomadic pastoralists. They lived on the fringes of the centres of higher culture and not only were they more mobile but they had a greater capacity for war. Thus the Bedouin preyed on the settled civilisations of Mesopotamia and Syria and the warlike tribes from north and east of the Danube and the Dniester preyed on the Danubian peasants.

In an agricultural community the value of the land lay in the amount of labour that was available for its cultivation, so that women, the traditional cultivators, were obviously as socially important as men. The wealth of the pastoralists, however, was accounted by the numbers of their flocks and herds, and their social organisation became patriarchal, aristocratic and predominantly male, for it called for a leader who was responsible for choosing new pastures and planning tribal raids.

Within the next few generations the Beaker and Battle Axe

people had emerged, producing a strain which was round-headed like the Beaker people but with the heavy build of the Scandinavians. The Beaker strain seems to have been predominant, and in Britain this mixed race is still called Beaker, but to avoid confusion it seems simpler to call them the Round Barrow people.

These people first reached Britain about 1800 B.C. They landed in the Thames estuary, the Wash, the Humber and along the east coast of Scotland, ranging as far as Ireland and the Orkneys, and they soon became dominant throughout much of England and Scotland.

They remained, for the most part, nomadic herdsmen and ofen lived in tents, although they also had small circular huts. Although their principal weapon was the stone battle-axe, they had a knowledge of the advantages of metal and were soon in contact with the smiths of Ireland and the Scottish highlands, who supplied them with small bronze weapons—axes, awls and daggers—which they used in addition to their stone knives and arrowheads, thereby establishing the British Bronze Age, although for several centuries to come bronze was to remain rare and costly.

They wore linen and woollen clothing, fastened in the Mediterranean fashion with conical buttons, which were sometimes made from Yorkshire jet, and their chiefs wore ornaments of Irish, Welsh or Cornish gold. Their bell-shaped beakers were in all probability drinking vessels for some kind of fermented liquor, but otherwise we know little of their social life. They did not practise communal burial but buried their dead singly, in a crouched position, with a few weapons and ornaments and invariably a beaker. Occasionally these burials were grouped in cemeteries, but more often they occur singly, the grave being surmounted by a hemispherical cairn of stones or of earth, the characteristic round barrow, which was sometimes built over a circle of posts or even a dwelling place which was perhaps the dead man's house. Although the burials were single, the same mound was sometimes used more than once.

Like all pastoralists, their religion was not concerned with the Earth Mother cult and the Vegetation God of the farmers, but with the heavens and the powers of the sky, the sun and the storm. The Sky God was the creator and supreme ruler of the universe. With the advance of the pastoral culture and the development of the warrior tribe, the Sky God tended to become personified as a celestial hero and chieftain, but the Sky God of the warrior peoples is, above all, the god of the thunderbolt and the storm. He is the Aryan Indra and the Scandinavian Thor.

The Round Barrow people left behind, in the megalithic tradition of their Beaker ancestors, the remains of two of the finest prehistoric temples to be found not only in Britain but in the whole of Europe—Avebury and Stonehenge.

Avebury, near Marlborough, was originally considerably larger than Stonehenge, though far less of it has survived. The temple is comprised of two sets of concentric circles of huge monoliths, each weighing several tonnes, placed side by side. These are surrounded by another ring of stones which, in its turn is surrounded by a ditch, embanked on its outer edge to a height of seventeen metres above the bottom of the ditch and enclosing an area of nearly twelve hectares.

From the inner temple an avenue of stones leads down to the river Kennet and then to Overton hill, where it ends in a small sanctuary.

Stonehenge, on Salisbury Plain, better known than Avebury, was approached from the river Avon by a road flanked for more than two and a half kilometres by banks and ditches. The temple was designed with an enormous outer circle of thirty monoliths which were originally joined by flat lintel blocks, held in position with tenons and mortices carved in the stones: and within this ring was an inner circle of smaller, separate monoliths, which enclosed a horse-shoe shaped sanctuary composed of five colossal trilithons. Within this was another horse-shoe shaped arrangement of smaller stones, inside which rested the altar stone, which was placed so that the priest, looking back along the axis of the horse-shoe, faced the point where the sun would rise on midsummer's day.

Little else is known of these temples, apart from the fact that they were built about three thousand five hundred years ago, by the Round Barrow people during the early part of the British Bronze Age. They are fascinating examples of a combination of the megalithic tradition of the Beaker strain, derived from the western Mediterranean, and the enclosing earthwork style of the eastern Battle Axe people, but how the huge stones were handled and moved, some from as far away as the Pembrokeshire hills, remains a mystery.

Several other examples of this kind of embanked sanctuary

have been found in Britain, though none so impressive as Avebury and Stonehenge. Woodhenge, not far from Stonehenge, was of a similar design, though it had been built of wooden pillars instead of stone. It was composed of a bank and ditch enclosing six concentric ovals of posts, planned to face the sun along their long axis. Other sites have survived at Arminghall near Norwich, in the Mendips, Cornwall, Derbyshire and the Orkneys, and the circles of standing stones to be seen on the moorlands of Cornwall, Somerset and Wales were also connected with the religious cult of the Bronze Age, which means that the religion was widespread throughout the country.

Never before can the people of Britain have seen such huge buildings. They must have come from miles around to gaze up at them in bewildered awe, and when the power of the priesthood reached out to them they were probably compelled, either from curiosity or fear, to stay and worship. This could have been the first time in their history that Britons had congregated in such large groups. Now they were not only doing the same things in their daily lives but accepting the same beliefs, imposed on them by a people who had gained an ascendancy by conquest and by imbuing themselves with a spiritual significance. They were having their first taste of indoctrination.

North of the Thames the inhabitants settled down peacefully enough, engaged in a little farming but still mainly stock-raisers, while some settled along the trade routes to the north and acted as middle-men for the Scottish and Irish smiths, distributing gold necklaces, gold and bronze ear-rings and other jewellery, some of which reached Denmark, north-western Germany and France. They made little advance in the manufacture of bronze implements, and their flat axes, small daggers and halberds were not outstandingly more efficient than the oval flint knives and other stone tools and weapons which they were still using. Nor was their pottery of any particular interest. They still buried their dead in round barrows, with vessels of food, stone and metal implements and jewellery, but occasionally the corpse was placed in a coffin made from a hollowed tree-trunk, like a dug-out canoe, reminiscent of the Egyptian idea that the passage to the next world was to be by water. The Scandinavians also accepted this concept and ultimately developed it into the elaborate and splendid Viking ship-burials.

In the south of England, round about 1450 B.C., there was an-

114

other arrival on the Wessex uplands of strongly-armed warriors who came, this time, from Brittany. Their numbers were not great but their armour was effective, and they soon established themselves as a ruling aristocracy, continuing a pastoral way of life but introducing improved methods of bronze working and many more foreign luxuries, from as far afield as the Near East and eastern Europe, for it was at this time that the Myceneans were extending their trade into Europe.

Their agents had penetrated the Danube for the metals of central Europe. They had reached the Baltic by the amber route from the head of the Adriatic and the Po valley to the Brenner Pass and the river Elbe. From the western Mediterranean and across France to Brittany they had reached the tin of Cornwall and the gold of Ireland.

In central Europe and in southern England blue faience beads, weapons and pottery, all of Mycenean origin, have been found, as well as less tangible results of their influence, in the way of ideas, motifs of decoration and techniques.

In the shaft graves of Mycenae have been found necklaces of Baltic amber in a crescentic form which was distinctively British, suggesting that the raw amber had been imported first to Britain and there manufactured. A small amber disc found in a grave at Knossos is similar to six which were found in a Wiltshire barrow. Faience beads from the eastern Mediterranean have turned up in at least thirty-five Bronze Age burials in southern England, while in Cornwall, near the Bodmin tin mines, a dagger was found which must have been made in Greece some time between 1400 B.C. and 1300 B.C. Additions may well have been made to Stonehenge at this time, and on one of the stones the outline of a Mycenean dagger was engraved.

The Phoenicians were now becoming important traders. They came from the region of the Persian Gulf and made their way across Arabia to Syria, establishing themselves in Tyre, Sidon and Byblos, cities of Akhnaton's lost empire, about 1300 B.C. They sailed westwards through the Mediterranean and the Straits of Gibraltar, exploring the coasts of Spain and Portugal. By 1200 B.C. they had founded the trading post of Lixus on the Atlantic coast of Morocco, and a century later Utica on the coast of Tunis, but it was not until 813 B.C. that Phoenicians from Tyre founded Carthage.

In the meantime the Mycenean civilisation had foundered,

overwhelmed in 1100 B.C. by the Dorians, barbarian invaders from north of Macedonia who occupied the Pelopennese and part of Asia Minor and brought about the final destruction of Troy.

This period of history in the Aegean and the Near East is obscure and a time of terrible violence and confusion. It was the beginning of the Dark Ages not only for Greece but for the entire civilised world. The Hittite Empire collapsed, overthrown by the Phrygians of western Anatolia, who had originally come from Thrace. The barbarous Chaldeans infiltrated into Babylon. Assyria held power in Mesopotamia through bloodshed and savage cruelty.

In mainland Greece the Dorians absorbed much of the accumulated knowledge of the eastern Mediterranean and by 500 B.C. had built Athens, heralding the days of Classical Greece, of Aristophanes, Socrates, Aristotle, Hippocrates and Alexander, all of whom lived during the fifth and fourth centuries B.C.

By the seventh century B.C. the Etruscan civilisation was established in Italy, to the north of a small town called Rome.

In Bronze Age Britain the years from 1500 B.C. to 1000 B.C. were comparatively uneventful—an interlude during which a characteristic British culture was established, compounded of all the different elements which had arrived during the previous thousand years and those of the indigenous survivors, although the newest arrivals, the Wessex chieftains, were no doubt the dominant class, using their stronger weapons to good effect against any who may have threatened their supremacy. These armaments included daggers with hilts which were sometimes beautifully inlaid with gold, but blades made more dangerous by being strengthened with a strong middle rib and more firmly fixed in their hafts. They carried heavy, spherical stone maces and their arrows were tipped with delicately made barbed flint heads.

In full dress, they were resplendent with gold jewellery and they used large quantities of amber, which they imported from the Baltic, some being made into beautiful ceremonial drinking vessels.

These Wessex rulers still buried their dead in round barrows, a custom which had been widespread in Europe, but in Britain two new forms emerged, mainly on the chalk uplands—the bell barrow, in which the hemispherical barrow is separated from its surrounding ditch by a level platform, and the disc barrow, in which the barrow itself is very small and the circular ditch, embanked on its outer rim, is the dominant feature of the general plan.

A number of these burials have been found near Stonehenge and Avebury, which suggests that the temples were still regarded as holy places, but little else is known of their religion or priesthood.

Bodies were still sometimes inhumed but now cremation became more usual, the remains at first being placed in a wooden coffin or laid on a wooden platform, with a profusion of ornaments, tools and weapons. Then funerary pottery urns came into use, to receive the ashes of the cremated, and the people of this middle period of the British Bronze Age, from about 1400 B.C. onwards, were known as the Urn people.

The custom of burying the dead in this way had spread from Anatolia to Hungary and then gradually westwards, After the collapse of the Mycenean metal market, bronze became less valuable and far more was available. The Urn people grew prosperous in the exploitation of this situation, manufacturing more bronze implements for general use and exporting to other parts of Europe, particularly Scandinavia.

In Europe they reached southwards to Italy, while north of the Alps Celtic-speaking Urn people who claimed to have been descended from the Greeks of the Trojan wars, who had escaped westwards at the beginning of the Greek Dark Ages, were spreading as far west as Catalonia and northwards through France to the southern shores of Britain.

Here, as their numbers expanded by natural increase, they pioneered much of the country which had hitherto been uninhabited because of the poverty of the soil. They spread into Yorkshire, Cheshire and the Pennines, and crossed from Scotland to Ulster. Far fewer possessions accompanied their Urn burials, which suggests that by now there was a radical change in the belief of a continuance of physical life after death.

Though they were still in the main pastoralists, the Urn people practised a small amount of agriculture, but it remained for the most part the simple hoe cultivation undertaken by the women, who also made the funerary urns. Their dwellings were wooden huts or more solid buildings of dry stone walling, often built in a group and surrounded by a protective wall. On Dartmoor a few impressions of their small square fields and the sites of their

117

huts have survived, but in the more fertile lands the traces of the Urn people have long since disappeared under the plough, except that in places, as, for example, the Thames valley, observers from the air may even yet sometimes catch the shadow of a ring ditch which may once have enclosed one of their little settlements.

The women wove the sheep's wool into fine cloth and also grew flax from which they spun and wove linen. Although no complete articles of clothing have survived, in water-logged coffins of this period which have been found in Denmark, enough has remained to give an indication of the style of dress the British Urn folk were likely to have worn—long cloaks for both men and women, with knee-length kirtles for the men and jackets and skirts for the women. Both wore a certain amount of jewellery, though few of them could have afforded the beautiful ornaments of Irish gold worn by the Wessex chieftains.

For most of the population of Britain life continued at a slow, unchanging pace. The forests were still places to be feared, dense and dark, with an almost impenetrable undergrowth, haunted by bears, wolves and wild boars. Roads were still only the beaten tracks. There were ridgeways, such as the Berkshire Ridgeway, over the tops of the hills, used by the stone workers in their search for flint: the narrow ways over the lower slopes, such as the Icknield Way; and the ancient hollow ways, used by so many generations that the soil had been worn away, leaving steep-sided banks on either side of the track. Only in the fens and the west country was there any attempt at road building, and here they built timbered causeways over the marshes.

By about 900 B.C. new generations of Celtic-speaking peoples arrived in Britain from Europe. At the same time there was, in Europe itself, pressure from a westward drive by German tribes from the north and Scyths from the east. The Scyths were horse-riding steppe nomads from central Asia who had been driven westwards from north China, prabably by emperors of the Chou dynasty, after they had been plundering the border villages of the empire.

The repurcussions were world-wide, for Celts now began to cross from north-west Germany to northern Britain and Ireland. Others came from northern France to the coasts of Kent and Sussex. Their arrival marks the beginning of the late phase of the Bronze Age in Britain, for as well as new techniques in bronze casting they introduced many new bronze implements, including a fierce, double-edged sword designed for slashing as well as cutting, a design which had first been introduced to central Europe from Asia Minor during the turmoils which brought about the collapse of Mycenae.

These Celts were agriculturists, and agriculture, which had been of minor importance in the economy of Britain since the days of the Windmill Hill people, now became of increasing consequence. Moreover, later arrivals of Celts brought with them a light plough pulled by a pair of oxen. Although it was capable of digging only a shallow furrow it was more effective than the women's hoe, and since it was driven by men her position as cultivator declined.

In the remoter northern parts of Britain the Urn people continued their pastoral life for a time, unaffected by the Celtic agricultural communities of the south, but throughout the next two or three hundred years increasing numbers of Celts arrived in Britain, driven from Europe by the incursions of fresh warrior tribes, amongst them southern Germans who had learnt from Italy the use of iron and who, after 700 B.C., were equipped with powerful iron swords. They first attacked the Swiss lake-side dwellers and thereby set in motion a wave of migrations of refugees, fleeing northwards and westwards throughout the continent.

Iron weapons had first been used by the Hittites, the earliest iron workers having practised along the southern shores of the Black Sea. Iron had been known to the Mesopotamians and Egyptians as early as 3000–2500 B.C. but the skills of the Black Sea workers were held secret by the Hittites, well aware that their much stronger weapons gave them an immense advantage in warfare. They exported a little iron, but only in the form of small ornaments and daggers, and it was not until the collapse of their empire in the twelfth century B.C. that the use of iron began to spread. In Palestine it was used for hoe-blades, plough shares and sickles, and from Syria its use spread to Cyprus, Greece and Europe.

The first iron-using civilisation of central Europe was known as the Hallstatt, after the type-station near Salzburg. The warriors who attacked the Swiss lake-side dwellers were part of this civilisation and the Celts to the west soon acquired the arts of iron working.

119

In southern Britain during the Late Bronze Age fresh waves of immigrants from Europe arrived and agriculture became increasingly important. More square Celtic fields appeared, none of them more than a thousand square metres and each enclosed by a low balk: and the pasture lands of these settled agriculturalists and farming communities were bounded by an embanked ditch, which was first marked out by the plough.

During these years, as bronze was so much more easily available, weapons of war—swords, spears and axes—were more numerous and also more effective, and the warriors used round shields, either of wood with bronze bosses or made entirely of bronze. Horses, too, were armoured, their accoutrements sometimes embellished magnificently with gold and bronze.

Tools and agricultural implements were better designed and more efficient, and for the first time large cooking cauldrons of bronze came into use, hung over the fire by their ring handles, a design which the Irish bronze-smiths copied from the Mediterranean. At the same time the Italian situla was copied—a bucket-shaped vessel, in the form of a truncated cone, and equipped, like the cauldron, with two ring handles.

Spindle whorls and loom weights appeared and also a more advanced type of upright loom.

Jewellery was lavish and gold ornaments were still being imported from Ireland, but very few were spared for the dead. There is, in fact, very little evidence of the religion of these Late Bronze Age people. They built no temples or massive tombs. They still cremated their dead and buried them in urns, which were usually placed in cemeteries or 'urn fields'.

In the west of England, where the barrow tradition still lingered, the urns were sometimes surmounted by a low round mound, but no offerings went with them and the urns themselves were severely plain.

Throughout the thirteen hundred years of the Bronze Age the population of Britain steadily increased in numbers and prosperity. In the north some of the old Urn folk continued their pastoral wandering life but in the south the country was scattered with neat, well-ordered farmsteads.

Then, by about 500 to 450 B.C. came fresh Celtic-speaking immigrants from Europe, bringing with them the iron of the Hallstatt culture.

CHAPTER TEN

The Early Iron Age in Britain

The year 500 B.C. is a convenient date for establishing the beginning of the Iron Age in Britain, but it was, of course, no sudden event. Immigrants from across the Channel brought influences of the Hallstatt culture almost a century before this and for many years to come the Hallstatt people in Europe were still using bronze for their weapons as well as iron.

In Europe the characteristic Hallstatt weapon was the long sword of bronze or iron, and great use was made of bronze for cups and vessels, helmets, shields and a variety of ornaments.

Their ancestry on the eastern steppes stood the Hallstatt people in good stead as riders, and although they probably did not ride into battle their horses did enable them to spread quickly over south-eastern and western Europe, and the number of hill forts and other military defences built at this time implies that their progress was a violent and militant one.

Their chieftains were not cremated and deposited in urnfields, but buried in timber chambers covered by large burial mounds; and throughout central Europe the remains of waggons have been found in their early burials, suggestive of the funeral carts of the Scythians. But by about 500 B.C. there were changes in Europe. The war chariot was introduced and in the grave of the Hallstatt princes these took the place of the old waggons, together with Etruscan and Greek grave goods, particularly wine flagons, which were now being traded over the Alpine passes as well as through the Rhône valley.

There were widespread movements of peoples throughout Europe at this time, partly caused by changes of climate. The

121

Eurasian steppes were growing drier and in the region of the Swiss lakes the rainfall was increasing, causing the level of the lakes to rise and inundate the villages. In the result there were fresh incursions of Celts to Britain, who introduced a fuller use of iron.

They came in waves from Holland and Belgium to East Anglia and north-eastern England, from northern France to the counties of the south and south-west. These Celts were artists but also a warlike, dominant people with a tribal organisation, and their advanced culture and material wealth soon enabled them to establish themselves as a dominating British aristocracy.

They introduced the use of the wheel, which they had adopted from the Etruscans, and applied it not only to carts and chariots, which were now seen for the first time in Britain, but also to the rotary quern for grinding corn, although it was to be many years before they made use of the potter's wheel.

In Europe the pattern of settlement had been the small village composed of several households living in rectangular dwellings, but Britain, despite the new cultural influences, retained its ancient circular house plan, and most of these houses were isolated farmsteads, as the one found at Little Woodbury, on the downs above the Avon river near Salisbury. It comprised a large, circular dwelling, built on a framework of posts, standing inside a circular fenced compound in which were the barns and byres, the granaries for seed, drying frames, winnowing pits, clay ovens for drying the grain and deep pits for winter storage.

A household of this kind cultivated probably about six hectares, perhaps two to two and a half each year. The sheep and cattle grazed on the downlands and the pigs down in the forested valley.

The Iron Age pottery was finer than anything Britain had seen before and included elegantly shaped bowls, sometimes decorated with incised simple geometric patterns, which were dipped in haematite and polished. These were probably the work of professional potters, while the women of the household continued to make the ordinary clay pots for general kitchen use.

Gradually, as the size of settlements such as Woodbury increased, they could be described as small villages: but with an increased population the warlike propensities of the Celts intensified. The warring factions built defensive hill forts, the best known in southern England being Maiden Castle, near Dorchester.

This was already an historic site, for during the third millennium B.C. about five hectares of the eastern end of this saddle-backed ridge, overlooking the wooded marshes where Dorchester now stands, had been occupied by late Stone Age people. They had built a few crude huts and, to protect the animals, a surrounding double ditch, and here they had lived for several generations until gradually they abandoned it.

In Neolithic times, about 2000 B.C., or perhaps earlier, along the highest contour of the ridge, a vast long barrow—the largest in England—was built, six hundred metres long, nearly two metres high and twenty metres wide.

Shortly after the building of the barrow, Neolithic people moved back to the enclosure, using the shelter of the long barrow for their kitchen fires: and here many generations lived peacefully. Neolithic potsherds have been found in the ditch, and in later levels relics of the Bronze Age Beaker folk, who arrived there about 1800 to 1700 B.C. But by about 1500 B.C. they had all gone, for by this time, with an improving climate, the peat bogs and swamps down below had grown drier and the ground had become capable of cultivation. So they moved down from the hilltop and for the next twelve hundred years Maiden Castle was deserted, except for the sheep which browsed on its pastures.

With the arrival of the Hallstatt Celtic immigrants, the Wessex people prepared for the worst and began to fortify Maiden Castle. They extended the area to about six and a half hectares and enclosed it with a wall of earth and chalk, three to four metres high, retained by wooden posts, beyond which they dug a new ditch seventeen metres wide and seven metres deep.

The fortress had double gates at the eastern end and a single gateway to the west, and inside were built small dwellings and cattle pens.

However, no attack came, and once the alarm was over the walls were allowed to fall into disrepair. The population continued to live there, and a hundred years later the settlement was enlarged by another eighteen and a half hectares, the walls being reinforced and barbicans built over the gateways.

As agricultural Britain slowly moved into its Iron Age, the Greeks were building Athens, and the little town of Rome, first built on its seven hills in 753 B.C., was gathering strength and importance, at the expense of the neighbouring Etruscans.

The Etruscan civilisation evolved in Italy, between the Arno and the Tiber, about 700 B.C. Influenced by the Phoenicians, the Cypriots and the Greeks, the Etruscans derived their wealth from the copper, iron and tin deposits close at hand and from their superb skill in metallurgy. They lived in self-governing cities and attained a high level of civilisation, with a written language, their wealth being evident in the furnishings of their massive tombs—vaulted or domed stone chambers which were covered with mounds of earth. The walls of the tombs were painted, and the funerary offerings included beautifully wrought gold jewellery, statuettes, ivories, urns, mirrors and Greek vases.

In Europe the Celts were expanding rapidly, and between 450 B.C. and 350 B.C. their warriors descended the Po valley, attacked the Etruscans and burnt Rome. They pressed on to the east, fought the Macedonians, attacked Delphi and did not stop until they had reached Asia Minor, where they eventually settled, and were known as the Galatians.

Not long after these south-eastern drives, Celts were also turning westwards, some crossing the Channel into Britain. During the century or more since their Hallstatt ancestors had arrived in Britain, the Celts had evolved a new culture, known as La Tène, a result of their contacts with the Etruscans and the Greeks, for between their fierce forays there had been periods of relatively peaceful trade, the Celts sending metals, furs, amber, salt and slaves to the Mediterranean, in exchange for pottery and bronze wine vessels and also quantities of wine, for which the Celtic chieftains had more than a passing fancy.

La Tène is at the eastern end of Lake Neuchâtel, and here a number of votive deposits of bronze and iron objects were discovered. The culture seems to have originated in the Rhineland and almost at the same time appears in the Marne. Here the grave goods of the warriors reveal a new decorative art style of outstanding beauty. It is an abstract art compounded of the Greek palmette, tendril and leaf motifs, which reached the Celts of the Rhineland with the wine trade, and the strange, stylised, barbarian art of the Scythians.

It was adopted by the aristocratic warrior society of Europe and adorned their armour and long shields, their spears, helmets, harness mounts, chariots and the jewellery of their women, all wrought in bronze, gold and silver and inlaid with enamel.

This art style was at the same time both attractive and repellant. Full of contradictions, it was refined in conception and workmanship; it differed enormously from Greek art, which was on a human and understandable scale, and it was the first great contribution made by a barbarian people to European art.

But when the people of Britain faced the arrival of the La Tène Celts during the third century B.C. they were more concerned with defending themselves than admiring the invaders' art, and they began hastily to build defensive ditches around their villages and strengthen their hill-top forts, as well as building many new ones, as was happening at this time throughout all Europe, from Iberia to the Carpathians.

In Britain, as in Europe, many of these forts were large enough to give pasturage to the flocks and herds. Stanwick, in north Yorkshire, was exceptional, for it eventually enclosed 340 hectares, with nearly ten kilometres of ramparts and ditches. Maiden Castle enclosed 18 hectares, Y Corddyn in North Wales fifteen hectares, Eildon Fort in southern Scotland sixteen hectares, with some three hundred circular, timber-framed houses; and south of the Humber a hundred and fifty hill forts have been recorded, each enclosing more than six hectares.

With their steep-sided, surrounding ditches and high ramparts strengthened by banks of chalk and earth, they were immensely effective, and in the south-east of Britain the La Tène invaders found only a few footholds in Sussex, Wessex and East Kent, but in East Anglia a group established themselves strongly, to found the royal line of the Iceni, and in east Yorkshire the Parisi gained a strong dominance over the native population, while in Scotland they were able to spread over the lowlands from east to west.

The upper crust of La Tène society was aristocratic and luxurious, both men and women dressed in long woollen cloaks with a wealth of bronze, silver, gold, coral and jet jewellery. The chiefs carried iron-bladed daggers with bronze hilts, often worked into a stylised human form, short iron swords in elaborately engraved bronze scabbards and oval wooden shields with bronze mountings. Yet they still lived in their primitive round huts and buried their dead in small, round barrows, although by this time the chieftains, at least, were interred with all their jewellery and weapons, and sometimes their chariots, though seldom with their valuable horses.

The Witham sword, dredged from the river Witham, is an example of their magnificent metal work. The sword is iron and the scabbard of bronze, worked into a fascinating pattern of scrolls, suggesting the gentle breaking of small waves on a sea-shore. The Battersea shield belongs to a much later date of the La Tène culture, perhaps the first century A.D., but this again is a splendid example of their bronze work with its curvilinear decoration and red enamel inlay of the studs, the arts of enamelling having come originally from the Caucasus.

During the early part of the La Tène invasions of southern and eastern England, there were also invasions in the south-west, where trader warriors from Brittany, the Veneti, were making a new bid for Cornish tin. Pytheas, the Greek explorer, who visited Cornwall in about 325 B.C., left a description of this industry. "The inhabitants of that extremity of Britain which is called Belrion both excel in hospitality and also, by reason of their intercourse with foreign merchants, are civilised in their mode of life," he wrote. "These prepare the tin, working very skilfully the earth which produces it. The ground is rocky, but it has in it earthy veins, the produce of which is brought down and melted and purified. Then, when they have cast it into the form of cubes, they carry it to a certain island adjoining Britain, called Ictis.* During the recess of the tide, the intervening space is left dry, and they carry over abundancy of tin in carts ... From thence the traders who purchased the tin of the natives transport it to Gaul, and finally, travelling through Gaul on foot, in about thirty days bring their burdens to the mouth of the Rhône."

The hospitality of the Cornish tin miners seems now to have been abused, for the invaders appear to have landed with little opposition and then built curcular forts for their own defence, such as Chun castle.

During the first century B.C. the Celtic civilisation grew increasingly warlike and in the south-west, by way of the tin route from the western Mediterranean, arrived a new weapon—the sling. The fortresses had to be adapted to deal with this new hazard and at Maiden Castle, for example, two new lines of mounds and ditches were added, in order to put a greater distance between the attackers and the attacked, for the sling stones had a range of two hundred metres.

In Somerset, at Meare and Glastonbury, the remains of two villages of these dangerous days have survived. For safety they were built in the marshes, on artificial islands made of logs,

* Ictis is almost certainly St. Michael's Mount.

stones, clay and brushwood, held in place by deep-set timbers, the upper parts of which formed a palisade. The lake village of Glastonbury has been wonderfully preserved in the peat. It covered about a hundred square metres and at one time must have supported some sixty round huts of timber and wattle, with thatched roofs, each hut having a stone or clay hearth in the middle of the floor. On the higher ground surrounding the village the Glastonbury folk cultivated their corn and vegetables and grazed their cattle. They had canoes for fowling expeditions in the marshes, and much of their life can be told from the relics which have survived in this strange, isolated but secure community of the first century B.C. The carpenters, as well as making the platforms and houses, made wooden vessels on a lathe and carved ladles and handles for iron implements such as sickles and bill-hooks, while the iron smiths forged saws, chisels and gouges. They still used a good deal of bronze, and amongst the finds was a magnificent bronze bowl. The women had small bone combs for their yarn threads and bone bobbins for their weaving. They had adopted the rotary quern, but their pottery, which included bowls and round jars, was still hand-made, beautifully decorated with incised La Tène patterns.

Glastonbury seems to have been a trading centre, importing Cornish tin, lead from the Mendips, shale from Dorset, glass beads and amber from the Continent and iron from the Forest of Dean, and some of the iron was used as currency, which circulated throughout much of the south-west and Wessex, in the form of long flat bars of a standard weight, pinched in at one end and suggesting the form of a sword blade.

About 75 B.C. there was yet another invasion of south-east England by Belgic tribesmen from the Low Countries. These Celts practised the La Tène culture and spoke Celtic, but there was a German strain in their ancestry. They fought from the chariot with sword and spear, seldom using the bow and arrow. Swords were by now long and narrow and sometimes of tempered steel. In battle the warriors were naked but like the Picts and the tribes of eastern Europe, the Thracians, Dacians and Scythians, they painted their bodies.

This was a time of the greatest turbulence and bloodshed Britain had ever known, for the Belgae pressed relentlessly through the country, seeking ever more territory. With their excellent iron tools they began to clear the forests and put the ground under

127

cultivation. For this they adopted a heavy, wheeled plough strong enough to cut the sod and turn it into deep ridges, but on the heavy clays of the valleys they often had to yoke eight oxen. This, in a small square field, was an unwieldly process, so the Belgic ploughmen now made their fields very long and relatively narrow, in contrast to the earlier Celtic square fields.

With the shifting scene of cultivation, tribal centres now tended to move from the fortified hill-tops to the lower ground. On the Essex Colne, Cunobelin—Shakespeare's Cymbeline—who came to rule over all south-eastern England, founded the first Colchester, close to where the Roman city of Camulodunum was to arise, a barbarian settlement of round huts behind a rampart and ditch where, nevertheless, amphorae of wine and beautiful Italian and Gaulish pottery arrived, by way of the Colne, in exchange for corn, cattle, metals, leather, hunting dogs and slaves.

Very little is known of the Celtic religion. It was fundamentally a form of animism and they paid tribute to the gods of springs and rivers, mountains and forests. Votive offerings of bronze and iron have been found in lakes and pools at La Tène, and at the Giants' Springs in Czechoslovakia a bronze cauldron containing more than a thousand bronze and iron votive offerings of middle La Tène date has come to light. Similar offerings have been found in lakes and pools in Wales, Norfolk and Scotland.

Their priests were the Druids, who presided over animal and human sacrifices, and the divinations by ritual murder. They also nurtured the cult of the severed head and the head-hunting practices of the warrior caste. Evidence of this cult have come to light in the south of France, as at Roquepertuse and Entremont, for example, where in large stone sanctuaries were found life-sized sculptures of human heads and niches in which human skulls had been placed and nailed into position. Human skulls often decorated the gateways of the hill forts. At Bredon Hill they were ranged across the lintel of the gateway which was to be destroyed during the troubles of the first century A.D., and skulls were also associated with the gods worshipped at the springs and wells.

The Druids used the Bronze Age Stonehenge as a place of worship, but the Roman historian Tacitus was to record that Anglesey was the strong centre of their religion and a mass of Celtic treasures has been found there in a bog—chariots, harnesses, swords, spears and a variety of ornaments—probably votive offerings. An iron slave-chain with five neck rings was also found there. The Celts do not seem to have used slaves in their households, although they exported them to the Mediterranean. They were no doubt prisoners of war, for whom the alternative fate was to be sacrificed on the altars of the Druids.

It was a cruel, barbarous religion, derived from the nomadic, pastoral ancestry of the Celts and, like all pastoral religions, it 'smelt of blood'.

As early as the second century B.C. many parts of the Celtic world in Europe were producing their own coinage, and the Belgae introduced a gold coinage to Britain, derived from the gold coins of Philip II of Macedon, although barter, as a means of exchange, was to continue for many years yet between crafts-men, traders and farmers.

On the crest of White Horse Hill, at Uffington in Berkshire, where there was a small Celtic fort, the famous white horse, a strange, prancing creature closely resembling the emblem on the Celtic coinage, was carved in the chalk, a hundred and twenty metres long and forty metres high. It could have been a tribal emblem or just a landmark for travellers, for the ridgeways leading from one Iron Age camp to the next are still discernible.

Whether or not its original significance was magical, it certainly acquired mystical properties in later years, for every seven years the intrusive grass was cleared from the chalk, to preserve the outline of the horse, and the 'scouring of the White Horse' be-came a festival lasting sometimes for two days, accompanied by the usual junketings.

The Giant of Cerne Abbas in Dorset is a little later, thought to be a Romano-British representation of Hercules.

By the middle of the first century B.C. the Celtic strongholds could be called small towns and the learned classes were gradually becoming literate, for British coins were inscribed with the name of the tribal ruler and the place of the mint in Greek and Roman characters, with a few in a rudimentary Celtic script, and weapons and pottery vessels also bore Greek and Roman inscriptions.

These were the signs of a dawning civilisation, yet despite this trend and their outstanding skill in metal work, which found a ready sale on the European mainland, the civilised world regarded them, with justification, as hard-drinking barbarians, cruel, blood-thirsty, most of them living in squalor and for ever at each other's throats.

By the time the Romans arrived, the Belgic tribes were

established in Kent, where the iron ore deposits were a source of continued power, and also north of the Thames in western Hertfordshire. In Essex and eastern Hertfordshire lived their sworn enemies, the Trinovantes, who watched their incursions into Northamptonshire and Oxfordshire with mounting fear and suspicion. In East Anglia were the Iceni, in the Cotswolds the Dobunni, in Cornwall the Dumnonii, in Wales and the Marches the Ordovices and the Silures, in Yorkshire the Parisi and the Brigantes.

CHAPTER ELEVEN

Britain and the Romans

The little republic of Rome had been born in 509 B.C., but it was not until the fourth century B.C., when the Celts were invading Italy from Gaul, that the Romans began a steady rise to power until they were dominating the whole of Italy. They gained control of the Mediterranean during the Punic wars of the third century B.C., and by 62 B.C. had annexed Syria and Crete.

Turning north-westwards, they began to expand into Gaul, to subjugate the Celtic La Tène people. Julius Caesar began the conquest of Gaul in 59 B.C. and by 55 B.C. he was chasing the Belgae across the Channel, as they fled to Britain.

From his own accounts, the first written records of British history, he landed on the Kent coast with ten thousand men, but his fleet was damaged in a storm off Deal, and the Belgae put up so stiff a resistance that he was forced to retire to Gaul with the remnants of his galleys. He reassembled his forces and struck again the following summer, in greater strength and with more success.

Caesar marched inland and captured a Belgic fort, probably Bigbury, near Canterbury, but the Belgae retired across the Thames to join forces with Cassivellaunus, the chief of the Hertfordshire Belgae.

Caesar sought help from the Trinovantes, which they gladly gave, though in later years it was to cost them dearly. Together the Romans and Trinovantes marched north-westwards and after weeks of bitter fighting discovered Cassivellaunus's fortress, possibly that at Wheathampstead, which they attacked and captured.

Caesar and Cassivellaunus came to terms. His people were to send an annual tribute to Rome, and once the details of the agreement were settled Caesar departed again, to finish his work in Gaul. Seven years later he had left north-western Europe for ever and had arrived in Egypt, where the Greek Pharaohs had been reigning since Alexander had freed the Egyptians from the Persians early in the third century B.C. Ptolemy XV had died, and his sister Cleopatra was reigning alone. She and Julius Caesar were married and journeyed to Rome to be proclaimed Emperor and Empress of Rome and Egypt, but Caesar was assassinated, and Cleopatra returned alone to Egypt with their son, Ptolemy XVI, only to meet with further tragedy after her marriage to Mark Anthony. Caesar's nephew Augustus defeated Mark Anthony at the Battle of Actium in 31 B.C. Anthony and Cleopatra committed suicide and the young Ptolemy XVI was put to death, so it was Augustus who became Pharaoh of Egypt and the first Emperor of Rome.

In Britain the bloodshed and strife, the struggle for power and wealth amongst the Celtic tribes was unabated. A boundary ditch —Beeches Bottom—more than thirty metres wide and ten metres deep, stretching from Wheathampstead to St. Albans, was built, either by the Trinovantes or the Belgae to protect one from the other. More Celts arrived from Gaul, fleeing from the Romans. About 50 B.C. came the Atrebates, under their chief Commius, landing at Chichester and settling to the west of the Belgae, in Sussex. The Belgae watched them jealously and built a fort where the city of Winchester was later to arise, as an outpost from which to keep the invaders in check.

The arrival of the Atrebates kindled afresh the flames which were never long subdued. Existing fortresses were strengthened and new ones built. For the next fifty years the three kingdoms of the south, the countries of the Atrebates, the Belgae and the Trinovantes, continued in bitter rivalry and ever-growing power, but the impulse for the fighting came from the chieftains, and the peasants continued their rural way of life, slowly bringing more land under cultivation from the forests. Only in times of extreme danger would they desert their farms to become part-time warriors with the regular soldiers.

In the year A.D. 10 Cunobelin, better known as Cymbeline, ruling from the Belgic capital at St. Albans, invaded the territory of the Trinovantes and captured their capital at Colchester. The royal family of the Trinovantes fled to Rome, to take refuge in the palace of Augustus.

Cymbeline held his new kingdom strongly. By A.D. 25 it stretched from Kent to the Iceni frontier in East Anglia and north-westwards to include Hertfordshire, Northamptonshire and Oxfordshire. To the west, the Atrebates cautiously entrenched themselves more strongly.

Cymbeline based his government on a freshly fortified Colchester, to which he began to attract new trade with Rome, growing rich with the sale of corn and iron-work, cattle and slaves to the Roman traders. It was probably at this time that the little Roman trading post was established, on the site where the city of London was to rise.

Cymbeline, at the height of his power, turned westwards to attack the Atrebates. Commius was dead but his descendants were still the ruling family. The Belgae battled victoriously through Sussex, Hampshire and Dorset, occupying Maiden Castle and bringing its defences up to date, with masonry platforms and towers and a fresh palisade of stone posts and hurdles along the top of the inner rampart.

Cymbeline died in A.D. 40, and with the loss of his generalship the fighting turned into uncontrolled savagery. Now it was the turn of the royal family of the Atrebates to flee to Rome, where the Emperor Claudius had succeeded Augustus.

Claudius listened to the story of anarchy in Britain and decided that the time was ripe to strike once more and bring this turbulent island under the complete control of Imperial Rome.

In A.D. 43 a Roman army, some 40,000 strong, of fighting men who were also engineers and craftsmen, led by Aulus Plautius, landed again on the coast of Kent. This time there was no turning back. The first objective was Colchester, which they captured within the first few weeks of the campaign, the vanquished Caratacys, son of Cymbeline, fleeing to the Silures of South Wales. Then began the conquest of the greater part of lowland England. By A.D. 47 Maiden Castle had fallen, the Romans advancing through a barrage of iron-shod arrows hurled from a ballista. They fought their way up to the eastern gate, burnt the huts built just outside it, and under cover of the smoke burst into the town and massacred the inhabitants. Then they dismantled the gates, tore down the palisades and left the survivors to bury their dead. Not long ago the remains of one of the defenders was found, with the iron head of a Roman catapult-arrow still lodged in his spine.

Within three or four years the Romans had gained control of the land south of the Humber and east of the Severn, but in the hills of Yorkshire and Wales they met stiff resistance.

Ostorius Scapula, succeeding Plautius as military governor, pursued the attack on Caratacys to South Wales. Caratacys fled northwards but was betrayed by the Queen of the Brigantes, and was deported in shackles to Rome, where he died.

Another ten years passed. Paulinus was now governor. He made another attempt to subdue the Silures in Wales and then marched north to rout the remaining Druids in their last stronghold in Anglesey. And while he was occupied in the west of the country, Boadicea, Queen of the Iceni, rode south from Norfolk to sack Colchester, St. Albans and London. Paulinus saved the situation only just in time, and Boadicea took poison rather than submit to capture.

Paulinus exacted such savage reprisals for this revolt that Nero, the reigning emperor, recalled him to Rome and his place in Britain was taken by Trebellius Maximus. By A.D. 81 Agricola was governor and the Silures and Brigantes, for so long the trouble makers, had settled down in comparative peace.

The first task of the Roman legions, once they had established themselves at Colchester, was to build roads for their advancing armies. The primitive ridgeways and harrow ways gave place to properly constructed roads, made on stone foundations. Watling Street ran from Dover to London and then up through the Midlands, with branches to Chester in the west and Newcastle and Carlisle to the north. Sometimes the new roads followed the old tracks. Akeman Street, for example, ran over part of the ancient Icknield Way, joining the Foss Way, built over the watershed of the Cotswolds, the old flint route of the Stone Age.

On either side of the roads, the dense oak forests and woodlands remained, where people could live in obscurity and isolation for a lifetime. Nevertheless, the new roads were an important first step in the unification of the country.

During his term of office Agricola reached as far north as the Scottish Highlands. He met the full force of the clans but then turned back, for in neither the wild north Britons nor the Celtic tribes of Ireland, still mainly nomadic pastoralists, did there seem any interest or profit for Rome.

Forty years later, in A.D. 122, the year after the Emperor Hadrian had visited Britain, work began on Hadrian's Wall, across the Tyne Gap from Solway Firth to the mouth of the river Tyne, to mark the northern limit of Roman occupation. It was a massive affair of stone, six metres high and nearly three metres thick, even in the least strong central portion, while at the eastern end and for many kilometres to the west it was seven metres thick. It had a battlemented parapet, with a defensive ditch on the Scottish side and a flat-bottomed ditch and bank—the vallum —on the south side. At intervals of a Roman mile, which was somewhat shorter than the English mile of 1.6 kilometres, turreted 'mile-castles' were built, square enclosures with a gated road straight through from north to south. A stairway led up to the ramparts and on either side of the roadway, between the north and south gates, were barracks for about fifty soldiers. There were eighty of these mile-castles, and in between each, at intervals of about 540 metres, were two watchtowers, built on the ramparts and approached by ladders, the look-out men keeping in touch with the mile-castles by means of smoke flares by day and fire signals at night.

South of the wall, seventeen fortresses were built as permanent headquarters of the legions, housing anything from three hundred to a thousand men. Excavations at the fortress at Homesteads, about half-way along the wall, have revealed the ruins of the storehouse, the governor's house, the barracks and the little shops, but many parts of the wall still stand, especially at the eastern end.

It was a remarkably effective barrier and although the Picts made a breach about A.D. 180, at a time when the garrisons of the wall were undermanned, it was quickly repaired, and while the rest of Britain absorbed the civilising influences of Rome, the Picts of the Scottish Highlands remained barbarians for several centuries to come, some of them hardly advancing from the Bronze Age.

The wall survived until after the 1715 Jacobite rebellion, when General Wade helped himself to some of the stones for his military road, and since that time many other people have taken away the Roman stones for building purposes; had it not been for these depredations the wall would probably still be complete.

In Britain the first Roman towns were built, logically planned and a sharp contrast to the haphazard Celtic villages, where many of the population still lived, under Roman supervision.

The civilised parts of the country were divided into five muni-cipalities, from which the government of the surrounding districts was administered, at Colchester, St. Albans, Lincoln, Gloucester and York, all of them former strongholds of British tribes. These regions were still separated to a certain extent by tracts of un-explored forests and undrained marshes, and the administration was difficult.

The rest of the Roman-occupied areas of Britain were divided into twelve cantons, based on the capitals of the old Celtic tribes, Canterbury, Chichester, Winchester, Silchester, Cirencester, Dorchester, Exeter, Leicester, Wroxeter, Caerwent, Caistor-by-Norwich and Aldborough.

And London became of increasing importance as a trading town, the centre of the road system and also of the financial administration of the country.

During the four hundred years of the Roman occupation their armies amounted to some 15,000 heavy infantry and probably about fifteen to twenty infantry cohorts, each up to a thousand strong, of men drawn from all parts of the empire, including no doubt some Britons, as well as Romans, while the native popula-tion of the country was rising to perhaps half a million.

The term of service in the Roman army was twenty-five years. After that time, the legionaries were made citizens of the Empire and allotted land as a gratuity. The wealthier Romans built country houses with large estates, parts of which were cultivated by their slaves—although this source of labour diminished as the fighting died down—and the rest rented to British farmers.

Before long Celts who had taken to life in the Roman towns and grown wealthy retired to similar country villas, but for the peasants life went on much as before. They still lived in their groups of small, round huts, and in the west country many had not yet adopted the heavy plough and long fields, nor the true potter's wheel introduced by the Belgae, which had become general throughout the rest of the country. They still ploughed their small, square fields with the older, light Celtic plough and made their pottery by hand.

Yet the Roman influence was incalculable. Druidism was exter-minated and the pagan gods of the Romans, more benevolent than those of the Celts, demanding not human sacrifice but pro-pitiation by the first fruits of the harvest, became associated with gentler Celtic spirits of the woods and streams, so that the Britons were easily able to understand and identify them with their own religious needs and emotions.

Although much of the independent, creative spirit of the abstract La Tène art was submerged in the craftsmen's attempts to copy the less imaginative art of the Romans, there were ample compensations in intellectual stimulus and material comforts.

The Roman knowledge of medicine, based on the work of Hippocrates, who had practised in Greece five hundred years earlier, was considerable, and men entering the profession swore the Hippocratic oath which still forms the basis of medical etiquette.

"I will use my treatment to help the sick according to my ability and judgment, but never with a view to injury and wrongdoing. Neither will I administer poison to anybody when asked to do so, nor will I suggest such a course ... I will not use the knife ... but I will give place to such as are craftsmen therein ... And whatsoever I shall see or hear in the course of my profession ... if it be what should not be published abroad, I will never divulge, holding such things to be holy secrets."

This thinking, new to Britain, was a preparation for the Christian doctrines which were to be introduced to the country after A.D. 363, when Rome adopted the Christian faith. The Pope, spiritual successor to St. Peter, was installed as Bishop of Rome, and in far away Britain the first Christian churches were built.

In material concerns, the well-planned cities were centred on a forum, with shops and administrative buildings. Most had a theatre and public baths, and although the houses of the humbler artisans were small and narrow, with the workroom often opening directly from the street, the richer houses were built with the rooms opening on to the central courtyards and had mosaic marble floors, painted plaster walls, with elegant appointments of pottery and bronze tableware and fine linen. Their sewerage and plumbing were efficient, with running hot and cold water and baths, and some houses had hypocaust heating, with hot air passing from a furnace to a space under the floor and through flues built into the walls.

At St. Albans, the Verulamium of Roman Britain, was the magnificent theatre, based on the pattern of the theatres of Classical Greece. At Silchester, built on the hill site of the original Celtic fort, were pagan temples, a forum and basilica and then the first Christian church, as well as stone dwellings for the upper classes, close to the wattle huts of the peasants.

At Bath the entire system of water heating and drainage have survived, as well as the baths. The healing properties of the spring at Bath were probably known to the Celts before the Romans arrived. The Romans directed the waters into a bath large enough for communal bathing, with a vaulted roof and surrounding colonnaded walk. Grouped round this building were the rooms of the ordinary Roman bath, the principle of which, like the Turkish bath, was to pass through steam-heated rooms of increasing temperatures and end up with a cold plunge and a massage.

The capital of Roman Britain was moved from Colchester to London quite early in the occupation. It was probably the site of a small Celtic hill fort—Llyn-Din, the Hill by the Pool, built on the north Bank of the Thames at the first slightly rising ground above the estuary, where the tributary of the Walbrook flowed into the main river.

The first London wall, three kilometres long, was built about the end of the second century A.D. There is no direct evidence that it ever ran along the river front, although containing walls were built here as the land sank and the river widened. The wall can still be traced and followed from Tower Hill to Aldgate, the gateway to Essex and Colchester, and then north-west-wards to Bishopsgate and Moorgate. West of Moorgate remains of the wall have been preserved in the underground car park and the north wall of St. Alphage's church. At Cripplegate was a Roman fort. The wall followed the south wall of St. Giles's churchyard and then, after Aldersgate, turned sharply southwards to Newgate, Ludgate and the river.

The population of Roman London, estimated at 30,000 rising to 45,000, was cosmopolitan, with an upper class comprising peoples of Italian and Gaulish descent, as well as Spaniards, North Africans, Danubians and Britons. There was a large Greek element among the merchants. The smaller tradesmen were mainly British and Gaulish, and the slaves mostly Britons.

Though Latin was little spoken in the provinces it was the common language of the official and commercial circles of London.

The toga was the formal dress of the principal Roman citizens, but mostly people wore a short tunic and hooded cloak.

They wore open leather sandals or boots and leather trunks. Their jewellery consisted of bronze brooches inlaid with coloured enamels, torques, bracelets, armlets and finger rings of bronze, silver, gold and jet, and their weapons were spears, javelins, daggers, swords, arrows and shields.

In their houses they had oil lamps and candlesticks, but mostly they used terracotta oil lamps, and where the house had no hypocaust heating they used braziers.

They had bronze kettles, jugs and frying pans, pottery mixing bowls, bronze and pewter tableware, although the glossy red pottery imported from Gaul was cheaper for most people, and the very rich ate from silver plate and drank from glass drinking vessels.

In the early days of the occupation the official religion of Rome was the worship of Jupiter, Juno and Minerva, though they were tolerant of other cults if these had no political implications. Later the state cult of the Empire was introduced in an attempt to bring about a closer union. The Emperor was now deified after death and during his lifetime his guardian spirit was worshipped.

Of the dozens of lesser gods there was little to choose between those of the Romans and the Britons, and at the root of most of the pagan worship was the cult of the mother-goddess. Dozens of religious emblems have been found in the foundations of Roman London or in the river—amuletic representations of the mother goddess to help in childbirth, little clay figures of Diana, Mercury, Apollo and Jupiter from household shrines, goddesses of springs and streams, phallic emblems to avert the Evil Eye, votive offerings of animals and also of human heads.

Gradually, however, coins were substituted for sacrifices, particularly in the foundation deposits of new buildings.

The cult of Isis, her husband Osiris and their son Harpocrates or Horus was established early in Roman London and also the cult of Cybele, the Great Mother Goddess of Asia Minor, whose lover Attis, a youth depicted in a Phrygian cap, was a god of vegetation who died and was resurrected each year. This was an orgiastic religion in which the priests were castrated.

The cult of Mithras was of a different order, a male secret society with high ideals of honesty, purity and courage, which numbered many of the wealthy officials amongst its members.

Mithras was the Persian god of light and his worship had

reached Rome through Asia Minor, where he acquired his Phrygian cap. The Mithraem of Roman London was discovered on the east bank of the Walbrook, during excavations to determine the exact course of the stream, and the treasures are now to be seen in the Barbican museum.

The central mystery of the Mithraic legend was the sacrifice of the Great Bull, the story being that before the creation of earthly life, Mithras, who was divine, though not the supreme god, was ordered to capture and kill the primeval bull. With his face averted in pity for the bull's sufferings, he dragged it to a cave and stabbed it to death; and from the blood and semen shed from the bull's sacrifice came all the useful life of the earth and the essence of goodness, conquering the opposing powers of evil and death.

Gradually the multitude of gods and goddesses came to be regarded as different manifestations of the same, all-embracing divinity, and paganism moved towards monotheism, but when Christianity came to London the guardians of the Mithraen buried their treasures to save them from destruction by the Christians, who were bitterly opposed to the cult, probably because, in so many details, Christianity and Mithraism were too much alike, even to the ceremonies of baptism by water and the communion meal.

But by this time the days of the Roman occupation of Britain and of the Empire itself were numbered. As early as A.D. 180 the Picts began fresh incursions into Britain. The garrisons at Hadrian's wall were reinforced, but the raids increased in violence and the defence of the frontier grew costlier every year.

By A.D. 193 there was civil war in Rome and dissatisfaction in the army throughout the Empire. And while they strove to put their house in order the despised Germanic tribes beyond their northern borders, barbarians whom they said were "men with nothing but voices and limbs in common with humanity", were growing in knowledge and wealth.

At the beginning of the fourth century, Constantius, father of Constantine the Great, fought a long campaign against the Picts, but it was not decisive, and a fresh threat appeared with the arrival of the Scots from Ireland, people descended from the Celts who had fled from Britain three hundred years earlier. They settled in western Caledonia and began their own raids on Britain.

At the same time the Germanic tribes from the north German plain—Angles and Saxons—began attacks along the east coast. Romans and Britons together built forts from the Wash to Portsmouth to protect the east and south coasts, forts such as Brancaster, Richborough and Pevensey, but the incursions grew deeper and stronger, and Anglo-Saxon landings began along the isolated shores of Northumberland. The vastly superior equipment of the Romans might have held them, but Roman strength was being dissipated, not only by the fighting on the Caledonian border, but also by threatening events beyond the eastern boundaries of their Empire.

In central Asia there had been a period of drought so prolonged that the Chinese had sent the marauding Mongol Huns driving to the west. As they approached the country of the Germanic Goths, the Goths in their turn approached the boundaries of the Roman Empire.

At the moment when Britain was being invaded from the north, north-east and east, she appealed to Rome for help, but the Romans were no longer able to send reinforcements. Instead they had to recall such legions as were left in Britain to help defend their crumbling Empire. As the Anglo-Saxons advanced through Northumberland, the Goths marched on Rome. In A.D. 410 Rome was captured and the Empire collapsed.

For Britain it was the beginning of the dark ages, as the country was overrun by Angles and Saxons. "Foes are they fierce beyond other foes and cunning as they are fierce; the sea is their school of war, and the storm their friend; they are sea-wolves that live on the pillage of the world" wrote a Roman of the time.

It was also the beginning of recorded history, yet it was from this period that one of our most precious archaeological treasures has come—the offerings from the ship burial of an early Saxon king of East Anglia, which were found at Sutton Hoo, on the east bank of the river Debden.

The ship had been hauled up from the estuary, buried in a trench in the sand and covered by a barrow. The timbers of the ship had all perished but the iron nails were still in position, and with the utmost care and skill archaeologists were able to measure the size of the original vessel. It had seen service at sea and was twenty-seven metres long with a five metre beam, having thirty-eight oars but no mast or sail.

No body was recovered from the ship. The position and size of the roofed cabin amidships could be discerned from the discolouration of the sand, and here the offerings had been placed. The gold had survived and a good deal of the silver, but the bronze was decayed and most of the iron rusted away, while hardly anything was left of the wood and leather. Nevertheless, the British Museum archaeologists, technicians and photographers were able to record, reconstruct and preserve a great deal, and establish that this was, in all probability, the funeral ship of one of the Saxon invaders who had established the Kingdom of East Anglia during the seventh century A.D., perhaps Aethelhere, who came to the throne in A.D. 654 but was killed the following year on a Yorkshire battlefield.

His family were Christian but his memorial was in the pagan tradition and the treasure, now in the British museum, included some of the most precious things to be obtained in seventh-century Europe and the Near East—silver tableware, gold buckles and clasps, a purse decorated with gold filigree and garnets, containing gold coins for his journey, a silver dish, sixty-eight centimetres in diameter, bearing the stamp of the Byzantine emperor Anastasius, which meant that it was already more than a hundred and fifty years old, a silver mounted drinking horn, silver and bronze bowls from the Near East, a Swedish helmet and shield, a hanging bronze bowl with enamelled decoration and magnificent jewellery of gold cloisonné work set with garnets and coloured glass mosaic, the jewellery being the work of East Anglian goldsmiths, whose genius was to develop into the superb Northumbrian art of the following century.

CHAPTER TWELVE

The New World

The civilisations of the Aztecs of America, the Incas of Peru and the Mayas of Yucatan and Guatamala provide a fascinating comparison with those of the eastern Mediterranean and western Asia. For many years the American civilisations were considered to be exotic growths which had been imported from the Old World after a slow diffusion eastwards, by way of Indonesia and the Pacific, bearing no relation to the cultures of the indigenous population of North American Indians.

Within the last fifty years, however, American archaeologists have been able to show that these civilisations, which the Spaniards discovered early in the sixteenth century, in varying stages of life or decay, were independent American developments of the indigenous American people and were not influenced by the social and economic transformations which were brought about in Europe, North Africa and Asia by the civilisations of Mesopotamia and Egypt, although they may have received a few cultural importations from Indonesia from time to time.

In both the Old World and the New, however, the pattern of growth was similar, coming about when climatic changes necessitated a changing way of life and a few men of outstanding ability discovered the processes of agriculture, which enabled them to establish a relatively stable way of life, supported by a reliable supply of food. Thereby they attained the leisure to develop the arts and skills of a civilisation.

The human race arrived relatively late in America. No fossil human remains have been found in the continent and it was Homo Sapiens who first ventured across the land-bridge from north-east Asia to north-western Canada. This was probably during a late phase of the Ice Age, when the land-bridge still existed, but the ice of northern Canada had temporarily melted sufficiently to allow a passage, though it was later to spread again, with the final period of severe ice.

These hunter-fisher folk, following their main source of food, the bison and the mammoth, made their slow migration across the inhospitable wastes of Siberia and entered the continent at the same time, a prodigious journey which may have taken place twenty-five thousand years ago or longer. The time is in doubt but it is certain that by about 10,000 B.C. these early hunters were living on the high plains of North America which stretch east of the Rockies to the highlands bordering the Mississippi basin. This region was wetter than it is today, and for hundreds of years they maintained their hunting life, chasing forms of horse, bison, camel, mastodon and mammoth, which are now extinct, with stone-headed throwing weapons.

Gradually the climate changed and as the plains became increasingly arid the game slowly disappeared, probably hunted out. The Indians began to move away from the centre of their first hunting grounds. As the ice melted from the north and north-east, some moved into Canada. Others went east, reaching Alabama, east Tennessee, North Carolina and Virginia and then turned north into the forests of Massachusetts and Vermont, where their diet was augmented by fish and a variety of plant foods. Those who moved towards the Rockies and the Pacific found themselves in increasingly arid steppe lands and had to adapt themselves to a subsistence of semi-desert vegetation and small animals. They still hunted the bison, antelope and mountain sheep when they could find them, but taught themselves to catch such creatures as foxes, coyotes, skunk and rodents with snares, traps and nets and also with darts tipped with small stone heads, which were propelled by dart throwers.

It was a hard, nomadic life. They moved in small groups and they sheltered in caves. Their possessions were few—digging sticks, fire-drills and darts, and nets and basketry which they had devised for carrying them. Yet as they adapted themselves to the desert environment, many showed little desire to try and find a more congenial habitat. Of those who did move, some migrated due south, and by 7000 B.C a few had reached the southern tip of South America and the Straits of Magellan, finding conditions as inhospitable as the desert home of their ancestors, yet they stayed on there.

Others on the way south, still practising their desert culture, stopped in Mexico, Central America and the northern part of South America: and it was here that they learnt to cultivate the indigenous maize plant and began a long period of steady development into highly organised societies.

Where exactly the cultivation of maize first began is not yet clear, but it was a direct development from people who had begun to gather it in its wild form, and the process of domestication seems to have occurred independently in four or five different parts of Mexico.

Along the narrow coastal plain of north Peru, where the Inca empire was to rise, the remains of people living between 3000 B.C. and 1200 B.C. have been found. They lived on fish, which was caught in Seine nets weighted by stone sinkers and with gourd floats, and also on shell-fish. They ate wild roots and fruit and where cultivation was possible, along the shores of the rivers rushing steeply down from the Andes, they had learnt to cultivate beans, gourds, squash and cotton, but not yet maize. They lived in sunken, one-roomed dwellings roofed with timber, and although they had no pottery they had learnt to spin and weave cotton into fabrics and mats, and had developed the art of basketry.

No more is known about them, but about 1200 B.C. there came a marked change. They had learnt to cultivate maize and manioc as well as squash and cotton, and had developed a primitive form of irrigation. They spread from the narrow coastal plain, which is only 160 kilometres wide, into the high plateaus of the Andes, and developed a fascinating culture, some elements of which seem to have come from Mexico, where a comparable society was developing.

The Peruvians took to living in permanent villages of rectangular gabled houses. They developed increasingly sophisticated religious beliefs which were associated with stone-faced pyramids ornamented with carved reliefs of animals, serpents and human beings. And in the scattered villages they built large communal centres in which stood a platformed temple and pyramids, built of earth, adobe or stone. These Chavin people were talented artists, and as well as their beautiful carvings and the spinning and weaving of textiles, they made pottery—strange ceremonial vessels in animal and human forms.

They had no hard metals, but discovered the gold and copper which abounds in Peru, and grew skilled in casting and gilding; and they alloyed tin with copper to make bronze, for weapons and helmets.

From the beginning of the Christian Era to about the middle of the seventh century A.D. the Peruvian civilisation developed and the population steadily increased along the coasts and in the highlands, where they practised terraced agriculture, cultivating a variety of plants such as the potato, the sweet potato, the pineapple and the tomato, none of which was known in Europe until after the Spanish conquest.

Their textiles, in both wool and cotton, were varied and attractive, including tapestries, brocades and gauzes, most of which were made by hand, although they had by now devised a loom, and the characteristic colours of their vegetable dyes were indigo, red, yellow, orange and brown. Their fine pottery, still in animal or human form, was polished and sometimes painted with scenes of warriors and the execution of prisoners of war, for by this time, towards the end of the first millennium A.D., they had organised themselves into states which were frequently at war with one another.

The population of the coastal region tended to concentrate in three large city states of which Chimu in the north, with its capital Chan-Chan, was the most important. Chan-Chan covered nearly three thousand hectares and was mainly comprised of ten or more large, rectangular enclosures, each about four hundred metres by two hundred and twenty metres and protected by massive walls fourteen metres high, into which the population was crowded, their existence made possible by the development of irrigation in the surrounding fields.

Organising themselves in this way, they may have been aware of impending danger, and by about A.D. 1000 it came. From the sparsley populated highlands of the Cuzco valley emerged the Incas, their name derived from their king, the Inca. They were a warrior people determined on conquest. Within the next four or five hundred years they had founded an empire which included the highlands of Peru, much of Ecuador, engulfing the state of Chimu, and ultimately reached to the south coastal regions of Peru, the highlands of Bolivia, northern Argentine and part of Chile.

The Inca régime was stern and uncompromising. Their ruler

was a god upon earth and he governed despotically with the help of a hereditary nobility, who were his blood relations, a priestly hierarchy and a host of especially appointed officials.

The state religion was the worship of a supreme god—a lord of creation—and also of the sun and moon, with an army of lesser gods, and it was conducted in stone-built temples which were furnished and lavishly ornamented with gold.

Here animals and crops were offered as sacrifices to propitiate the gods and bring well-being to the empire. In the early days, at times of crisis or calamity, such as the death of the king, women and children were also offered, but the practice of human sacrifice had been abandoned by the time the Spanish arrived.

The king had supreme power and through his officers every detail of the lives of the ordinary people was controlled and circumscribed. Here again the despotic autocracy seems to have softened as the empire grew older. At first the subject people were ordered to forced labour in the fields and mines, to road-making or the army: they were moved arbitrarily from one part of the empire to any other part where their labour was more needed, and even their marriages were arranged by Inca officials.

The empire was maintained by a remarkably efficient system of roads, which in some ways could compare with that of the Romans, but the Inca roads were narrow and rough, for they had no wheeled traffic to consider, and they ranged over the highlands and mountains as well as the coastal areas. Their only draught animal was the little llama, and mostly they used human runners. Over the deep ravines and swift flowing rivers they threw suspension bridges of thick lianas which were sometimes a hundred metres long, perilous-looking but sufficient.

Along the roads rest-houses and store-houses were established and, as with the Romans, the roads enabled the Incas to control a large empire of people speaking a diversity of languages or dialects.

As the Inca despotism softened with the passing years, the conquered were no longer regarded as slaves. Each family had its allotment of land to farm, with a home of its own and an adequate supply of food, but there was still a high degree of regimentation and everyone had to work.

The Incas had no writing but devised a system of knotted strings, the arrangement of the knots conveying such information as a message required. Their skills lay in their knowledge of plants and cultivation and their remarkable architecture. High up in the Andes they laid soil in terraces which they fertilised with guano, and in the lowlands they deflected rivers and dug irrigation canals.

They discovered the therapeutic properties of cinchona bark, from which they extracted quinine, and of the coco-plant, from which they made cocaine, and apart from these drugs they made an extremely potent drink called chicha and indulged in drinking bouts which could last for days.

At Cuzco, their capital, the supreme god was represented by a large flat plate of gold, suggestive of Akhnaton's conception of the god Aton, who was not the sun but the life-giving force which created the sun, but also at Cuzco there were temples to the more tangible gods, the sun and moon themselves.

The Inca empire was in full strength when the Spaniards arrived, but there was an inherent weakness in its structure, for although the king was the supreme ruler the laws of succession were ill-defined. The king had several wives and on his death the kingdom passed to one of their sons, but there was no law of primogentiture to say which one, so the stage was set for the most bitter feuds between half-brothers: and it was during one of these periodic turmoils that Pizarro landed in 1532. The Inca weapons of stone and bronze spears, clubs and bolas were no match for Spanish iron and gunpowder, and the Inca empire fell, although for several years Titu Casi, the last but one of the Inca rulers, held out gallantly and disdainfully in his mountain stronghold of Vilcabamba, a secret city built more than seven hundred metres above sea level, on the wild mountain ridge overlooking the grand canyon of the swirling Urubamba river, which protects the city on three sides.

Here, with its steep terraces of cultivation, are some of the finest examples of Inca architecture—houses, palaces and gardens, watered by stone conduits from nearby springs, which brought the water under the city walls to stone storage tanks, the semi-circular temple of the Sun, built of massive stone blocks of white granite, the sacred plaza, the granite stairway leading to temples where the mummies of long-dead Incas lay and a shrine with three vast windows looking across the canyon and the cloud-capped mountains beyond, to the setting sun.

Titu Cosi held court and parleyed with the Spaniards, main-taining the full panoply of his majesty, the diadem and plumed head-dress of many colours, the golden shield and lance, the silver breast-plate, the feathered garters with wooden bells. His warriors from the jungles of the Upper Amazon danced their war dances, and a carefully selected company of the Chosen Women of the Sun, including some of the languorous beauties from the coastal regions, where "modesty and chastity were unknown", tried, though it would appear in vain, to seduce the Conquistadores into a more temperate humour.

Tuti Cosi died and his brother Tupac Amaru, who succeeded him, was neither strategist nor diplomat. He was seized by the Spaniards and brought down to Cuzco, where, after a brief trial, he was put to death, with his wife and court.

In Mexico the civilisations of the Toltecs and Aztecs followed a similar pattern to that of the Incas, beginning with the domestication of plants to add to a diet of gathered plants and the produce of primitive hunting. This was succeeded by a period of experimentation and development of agriculture, so that by about 2000 B.C. there were settled farming communities in Mexico and an established village life, culminating in the establishment of large urban centres, over which a priesthood presided.

From 800 B.C. to 400 B.C., in the tropical forests and swamps of the Gulf coast, the Olmec people were the most advanced in Mexico, and at their centre of La Venta they built a ceremonial meeting place and a huge pyramid, connected with their strange religion. This was based on the creation myth of the union of a woman and a jaguar, which resulted in a race of werejaguars.

Jaguars appear over and over again in Olmec art, and at La Venta small representations of these sinister looking creatures, carved in jade and serpentine, have been found. The Olmecs also carved small human figures which had no indication of any sexual characteristics; but they all had fat, sulky looking faces. Some colossal basalt heads, up to three metres high, have been found, and they all bear the same forbidding expression, with downcast mouth, as the smaller figures.

Some of their jade axes and personal ornaments were carved with primitive hieroglyphs, which means that they were beginning to acquire a form of writing. These have not yet been deciphered, but may well bear some relation to those of the Maya people.

Little more is known of the Olmecs, except that they carried war clubs and weapons rather like knuckle-dusters, suggesting that the blessings of civilisation had already made them belligerent.

In the south of Mexico, while the Olmecs were reaching the summit of their powers, rose the Zapotecs, whose early culture had probably been derived from the Olmecs, and whose centre was at Monte Alban, where people speaking the Zapotec language are still living.

The buildings in Monte Alban have the characteristic Mexican features, the main plaza with the flat-topped pyramid and flights of stairs reaching to the upper platform, temples and dwellings. The earliest buildings date from about 350 B.C. to 100 B.C. and the later from 100 B.C. to about A.D. 950. These people also had a knowledge of writing and, in addition, they had devised a calendar, so that culturally they were more advanced than the Olmecs.

By the beginning of the Christian era there was a third centre of civilisation in Mexico, on the high plateau in the Valley of Mexico, where at Teotilhuacán, forty kilometres north of where Mexico City was to arise, stood the House of the Gods, the largest city America had ever seen, covering an area of nearly eight hundred hectares. It was a place of ceremonial pyramids and monumental buildings, with beautifully carved frescoes where, by the sixth century A.D., the population was about fifty thousand.

Their main god was the rain god Tlaloc, derived from the Olmec were-jaguar and his consort, the water goddess, who was especially venerated, since they had no irrigation system. But equally sacred in the hierarchy of the immortals were the sun god, the moon goddess and the feathered serpent, Quetzalcoatl, and they all had their places of worship, the stepped pyramid of the sun being the largest of all the buildings in Mexico at this time—two hundred and fifty metres long by seventy metres high—with the pyramid of the moon on a similar gigantic scale.

They were literate and dates were recorded, yet they were still in a stone age of culture, using quantities of obsidian for knives, spearheads and dart points.

The civilisation of Teotilhuacán lasted until about A.D. 600, when it fell to the Toltecs of Tula, but the Toltecs in their turn were overthrown by the Chichimees during the twelfth century, and the Chichimees soon succumbed to the Aztecs, who had arrived in Mexico Valley from the north. By 1325 the Aztecs had founded their capital city and ceremonial centre at Tenochtitlán, on two islands in Lake Texcoco.

Compared with the Toltecs and the Chichimees, the Aztecs were a fierce, cruel people with a rigid class system of serfs, free-men, officials, nobles and priests, and at the head of the hierarchy was a dominant, all-powerful, semi-divine king, the earthly manifestation of their fearful god Huitzilopochtli, who demanded human sacrifices for his propitiation.

The Aztecs exercised a ruthless domination over their weaker neighbours, who feared and hated them. When Cortes landed in 1519, therefore, they did nothing to help them, and after nearly two hundred years of supreme power, they quickly fell to the Spaniards.

In south-eastern Mexico the Mayas attained the highest of all the central American civilisations. Here again there were clearly defined stages of progress, beginning about 500 B.C. with their first agricultural settlements, which were based on the cultivation of maize.

By about A.D. 300 they had founded their first empire in the tropical rain forests, but by about A.D. 700 they had moved to the plateau of Yucatan, probably because they had exhausted the soil of their original sites.

The Mayans were a kindlier, milder people than the Aztecs, living in scattered, rural hamlets. Unlike the other Mexican civilisations, their religious centres, of which the most famous is Chichen-Itza, were peopled only by the priests and their attendants, and here the Mayans came to worship dance, pray and make sacrifices at the grey stone temples set on their stepped pyramids. The religion was similar in many ways to that of the Aztecs, a nature worship and deification of the sun and moon and the elements, and a supreme god, the Quetzal-coatl of the Aztecs, whom the Mayans called Kukulcan and represented as a feathered serpent.

There was little human sacrifice in the early dynasties, al-though it was practised during the later periods, just before the empire collapsed, at the time when it had come under the influence of the Aztecs.

The priests studied astronomy and mathematics. They had an intricate calendar system and had devised a hieroglyphic writing for recording outstanding events in the history of their people.

They carved these inscriptions on the walls of their ceremonial centres and also painted them on strips of bark cloth, but this was their only literature.

The hieroglyphs have not yet been properly deciphered, although several Maya dialects are still spoken in Guatemala, where some two million of their descendants still live.

At the height of its glory Chichen-Itza was a vast city, covering more than three thousand hectares. This included an older, abandoned city and a newer one built close by, comprising a nucleus of ten or twelve large temples and palaces, while the small, rectangular houses of the ordinary people were scattered about the surrounding countryside.

Chichen-Itza is well supplied with natural wells, the largest being the Sacred Well, a vast rock cavity more than fifty metres across at its widest point, which is approached by a stone causeway from one of the sacred pyramids. Into this well men and girls were thrown, in times of drought, as sacrifices to the Rain God, and one of the most dramatic feats of archaeology was early in the present century when Edward Thompson, the American Consul to Yucatan, decided to train himself as a diver in order to explore the depths of the twenty-metre-deep well and recover some of its secrets. He found skulls and bones of young girls and mature men, temple vases and incense burners, stone lanceheads and arrowheads, axes and hammer stones, copper chisels, discs of beaten copper, some of which were embossed with representations of the Maya gods, and a profusion of gold and jade ornaments, as well as scores of small golden bells, which were a favourite form of votive offering to the rapacious Rain God, who was believed to live at the bottom of the well.

Kukulcan, in the form of the feathered serpent, figures largely in the buildings at Chichen-Itza. From the base of the pyramid a feathered serpent is carved at each corner, curving from the base to the platform on which it stands. The pyramid is built in nine terraces and on each side run broad stairways up which the sacrificial victims were dragged to the topmost part of the temple, where they were slaughtered and their hearts held up by the priest, for the benefit of the watching worshippers below.

To the west of this pyramid was a large ceremonial court where, as in other Mexican ceremonial centres, a ritual ball game was played, a contest which occurred in many primitive societies from ancient Egypt onwards, and was associated with the mysteries of the death and resurrection cycle of nature. The ball game has survived in varying forms ever since, its early intention being to promote the well-being of the community by the continuance of the life cycle.

By the end of the thirteenth century the Maya civilisation came increasingly under the influence of the more violent civilisations of Mexico, the Toltecs and then the Aztecs, and the older it became, the rougher and more brutal it was. First came the human sacrifices. Then the losers in the ball game were sacrificed. The buildings of the later generations were smaller and less significant, like the late Egyptian pyramids of Nubia, and by the end of the fifteenth century, a generation or more before the arrival of the Spaniards, the kingdom had collapsed. The end may have been due to soil erosion, the silting of some of the supplies of fresh water or the over-clearing of the forests. Whatever the cause, the Maya civilisation crumbled and returned to the jungle.

American archaeologists have devised a different terminology for the American civilisations from that used in Europe and Asia. Thus, instead of the Palaeolithic, Neolithic, Bronze Age and Iron Age of the Old World, the New World cultures are known as the Lithic, Archaic, Formative, Classical and Post-Classical ages.

The American Lithic and Archaic correspond in a general level of achievement, though not of age, with the Upper Palaeolithic and Mesolithic of Europe, and the Classical and Post-Classical stages—at which all but the already-defunct Maya civilisation were interrupted by the arrival of the Spanish—had certain elements of the Old World Neolithic and Bronze Age civilizations, although they still lacked many of them.

Their tools and weapons were mainly of stone or wood, and they used a good deal of obsidian. They had no hard metals such as iron and their few copper and bronze tools were not strong enough for their monumental masonry and carving, for which they had nothing but stone tools. They had no wheel for vehicles or pottery, and their only beast of burden was the small llama, so that transport was mainly on the backs of men or by canoe.

Although their economy was based on agriculture, which included seed plants such as maize, beans, squashes and tubers, they had no plough, using only a digging stick and a hoe. They had no knowledge of stock-breeding and no milk-producing animals, the only domesticated animals being llamas, turkeys, muscovy ducks, guinea pigs and small, edible dogs.

Their knowledge and use of writing were very limited. The Aztecs possessed only a crude, pictographic form. The Mayas used their hieroglyphs only in connexion with their religious rites and ceremonial observances, while the Incas had nothing but their knotted strings.

CHAPTER THIRTEEN

Field Work

Against the background of these world-wide movements of pre-historic peoples, which make aggressive nationalism appear so stubbornly retrogressive, the work of the individual archaeologist may seem daunting, but wherever he may be working, a single find could well prove of immense value in helping to fill a gap in the long and complicated story of mankind.

For those who want to become professionals, there are degree courses at the universities, after which the best step is probably to an appointment at a provincial or national museum, but there are plenty of opportunities in the Ministry of Public Buildings and Works, the Royal Commission on Ancient Monuments and the Ordnance Survey.

In the countries of the Near East and eastern Mediterranean most excavations are now conducted by their governments. Before the last war, when excavations, as in Egypt, for example, were mostly financed by European and American millionaires, through their national museums, all the finds went first to the Cairo museum, where the directors selected all they required, the rest being distributed amongst the museums of Europe and America which had a financial claim. It was an expensive business, for in order to avoid pilfering, the workmen on the dig, sometimes amounting to several hundreds, had to be paid the current dealer value of anything they personally found.

In Great Britain, the bombing of World War II and the ever-deepening excavations for the foundations of ever-taller buildings has turned up a great deal of valuable material, particularly Roman and late Iron Age, but here speed is the essence of excavation, as large construction companies obviously cannot afford to hold up operations while the archaeologists have their day.

It is in cases like this that a band of trained amateurs, working under professional direction, can be of inestimable value.

There are training facilities for part-time workers at many of the universities, often provided evening lectures in the winter and excavation schools during the summer, where they can gain their practical experience, working with professionals.

Most counties in England and many in Scotland and Wales have their County Archaeological Societies, with winter meetings and summer excursions, and the Council for British Archaeology, formed in 1945, is the co-ordinating body, helped financially by the government, through the British Academy.

The Council for British Archaeology has some extremely useful publications, including off-prints of articles in the journals of the national and county societies and a monthly spring and summer calendar of all the excavations being carried out currently throughout the country.

Having decided on a spot where you would like to take part in excavations, the first thing you must do, on the principle of working from the known to the unknown, is to find out all that has already been written and recorded about it. The Victoria County Histories cover many counties, although the project of collating all the known relevant material was not completed, the work being taken over by the Institute of Historical Research of the University of London.

The archaeology division of the Ordnance Survey publish special period maps of Iron Age, Roman and Monastic Britain, and the English Place-Name Society publish county surveys. The Society of Antiquaries, the Royal Archaeological Institute, the British Archaeological Institute, the Prehistoric Society, the Society for the Promotion of Roman Studies, the Society for Medieval Archaeology, the Cambrian Association and the Society of Antiquaries for Scotland all publish journals, either once or twice a year: and your local museum, which is the best place for obtaining local knowledge, will be able to provide you with details of all these sources.

To equip yourself for the job, you should have a knowledge of the geology of the district, of the character of its agriculture and the nature of the fields over the last two thousand years; of ditches and earthworks, long and round barrows and other burial sites.

There is much of Roman Britain still to be discovered, for in many of their towns, which remained centres of settlement after their withdrawal, centuries of later building have almost eliminated all trace of their work, yet it has survived in numbers of walls and cellars. Moreover, many of the side and minor roads of their road system have still to be discovered and traced.

Some medieval villages have been entirely deserted or destroyed by disastrous fires, leaving no surface traces, except to the trained eye, while Henry VIII and Thomas Cromwell left many ruins, not all of which have been accounted for.

The sites of flint mines and mineral workings, particularly pre-Roman surface workings of copper, lead, tin, silver, gold and iron should be noted, and the Iron Age and Roman pottery works, for pottery is, above all, the most valuable dating medium.

For a regional archaeological survey of an area, the first step is to walk over the fields with a six inch to the mile Ordnance map, noting everything, the shape of the fields, the contours, hedges, ditches, trees, dwellings and any mounds which could be man-made. A survey will be helpful, either with a theodolite or, more simply, with a plane table and ranging rods; and an alidade or clinometer is useful, for measuring and recording the profiles of the site.

Aerial photography can highlight banks and ditches which might well be missed from the most careful ground observation, and the study of crops can help to give an indication of buried walls and foundations, for if seed has been sown over stone foundations the crop is markedly poorer and will ripen sooner. Conversely, if the seed has been planted over hidden ditches or pits, and therefore nearer to a supply of moisture, the crop will be noticeably taller and stronger than that of the surrounding areas.

Aerial photography, though so valuable, is expensive, and there are other devices for detecting buried sites. In passing an electric current through the earth between two electrodes, it will be found that water pits and ditches will register a lower resistance than the virgin soil, while walls and other forms of masonry will offer a higher resistance. A magnetometer reading will record the presence of such materials as iron and the iron particles present in burnt clay, and is therefore valuable in the discovery of pottery kilns, but one must remember that it is also sensitive to iron in other forms in the vicinity, such as the corrugated iron roofs of farm buildings and overhead cables.

Having located the promising site and once the work of excavation begins, a high degree of skill is necessary, for it is by no means easy, in most cases, to detect the different layers of deposits as they have been laid down by succeeding generations, and for any objects to have a meaning which an archaeologist can decipher, it must be found and recorded in its exact context. The safest method, where possible, is to dig a small vertical section, which will act as a guide and indicate what one has to look for, but one must take care, in doing so, that a large feature not discernible in a small exposure, is not destroyed. A stratified site will produce a succession of cultures, and when this succession occurs at several different places it is safe to assume a culture sequence.

Except in very rare conditions of peat, desert or deeply frozen soil, such as that north of the Altai mountains in western Siberia, where the frozen tombs of Pazyrk were found, most organic materials—wood, hide, wool, leather, linen, grass, hair— are perishable, only such things as stone, bone, glass, metal and earthenware surviving, so the utmost care must be taken with composite objects, parts of which have decayed, in order to deduce the original form.

Stratification may have been disturbed by burrowing animals, and the refuse pits, wells and deeply dug graves of later inhabitants of the site. Earthen floors of dwelling houses are difficult to identify and often show up better in a section, where the baked earth surrounding a hearth may give a clue.

Objects are left standing on floors and the stone threshold of a door or the socket stone on which the door pivoted may also give an indication.

The tells of the East give more clearly stratified sites than the perishable wooden huts of Europe, for once a wooden hut was abandoned, to be rebuilt, it was cleared to ground level and all traces of the original building disappeared, except for the post holes, discernible by a discolouration of the earth and perhaps a few remaining packing stones: stone houses, on the other hand, even those built without mortar, can last for hundreds of years, and the Neolithic village of Skara Brae in the Orkneys, with huts made from stones collected from the beach, built on sand and put together without mortar, have survived for 3400 years.

Apart from hoards and living places which have been hastily abandoned, the best finds are usually from pagan burial sites. In addition to the famous finds from the tombs of Sumer, Egypt and Crete, most of the Greek vases and Chinese portrait figures, prehistoric bronze armour and vessels were all found in graves.

A prehistoric grave may be a pit, trench or shaft, sometimes lined with mats, brickwork, wooden or stone slabs. A grave lined with stone slabs is known as a stone cist, a brick-lined grave is a brick cist. Short stone cists are lined with four slabs on edge and roofed with a fifth, and they are large enough only for a crouched burial. In Britain these are usually Bronze Age. Long stone cists are for the burial of extended corpses, needing more side and cap stones. Most of these are early Christian, but some are Iron Age.

Shaft graves lined with stone slabs often have a ledge in the side walls to support a covering stone, placed about sixty centimetres above the body.

Tombs, as opposed to graves, may be defined as any artificial receptacles for a body, either below or above ground, which are more elaborate than a simply excavated grave. These include subterranean chamber tombs approached by a sloping ramp, a stairway or passage, tombs built at the bottom of a shaft or at the end of a passage driven into the hillside.

Stake holes in the floor of a grave shaft indicate that some English chieftains had been buried in mortuary tents or huts, while in Scotland mortuary houses were built of wood or on a wooden frame, above ground, and then covered by a barrow.

The tombs of the megalith builders were burial chambers walled and roofed with great blocks of undressed stone or walled with coursed rubble masonry. By being covered with a cairn of stones or a mound of earth they were artificially put underground, but today most of the coverings have disappeared.

These megalithic tombs are grouped approximately into dolmens, composed of four uprights supporting a single cap stone, passage graves, where the burial chamber is wider and higher than the passage, and gallery graves, where the chamber is long and narrow, approached by only a shallow porch or antechamber of the same width.

The tholos or beehive grave of Mycenae is occasionally found in Spain and Portugal.

Chamber tombs are not exclusively prehistoric, for the Holy Sepulchre was clearly a rock-cut tomb. Most built tombs were covered by a barrow, but most barrows, whether long or round, did not necessarily cover a tomb but more often a simple grave or just the body, and some were enlarged at a later date to accommodate further burials.

A large unidentified artificial mound could, of course, be a Norman motte. These flat-topped mounds were the bases of their keeps, built at the side of the bailey or enclosure and surrounded by a rampart and ditch. Although most of the keeps were strongly built of stone, some of the early, temporary ones were timber constructions, of which nothing has survived.

A mound surrounded by a ditch, with a bank heaped on the outside could, on the other hand, have been a Roman signal station, which at one time had a wooden or stone tower in the middle. Ditches enclosing a relatively small area may be the remains of bell barrows, disc barrows, henges or causewayed camps. Roman amphitheatres were usually oval in plan, with a gap at either end, enclosing an area of about a hundred and twenty by seventy metres.

A ring of anything from seven to fourteen metres diameter, with a single gap and no surrounding ditch, could be an Iron Age or medieval hut circle, the bank, usually reinforced with boulders, being all that remains of the low wall of clay, earth or stones on which the conical roof once rested. It would have had a central hearth and perhaps a drain under the floor, running out through the gap.

Rectilinear enclosures are probably Iron Age or Roman cattle compounds. Most Roman camps, temporary or permanent forts, were built on rectilinear earthworks, with an entrance in the middle of each straight side, protected by a ditch and a bank, which was the base of the stockade. These are, of course, in marked contrast to the British hill forts, which were built on high ground with defensive ramparts and ditches following the contours of the hills.

A bank and ditch running on for a long distance, without apparently enclosing anything, could be an ancient boundary or frontier defence. In Britain the earliest of these are late Bronze Age and the others are medieval. The Grim's Dyke earthworks were probably Wessex tribal boundaries, and Offa's Dyke was an eighth-century frontier line, built by Offa, King of Mercia, stretching from the River Severn to the Wye, to hold back the Welsh tribes whom he had driven into the mountains.

The first Antonine wall of the Romans, from the Forth to the Clyde, and the earlier form of Hadrian's Wall were also earthworks of this kind.

The remains of Roman roads may look like linear earthworks, with low but wide banks flanked by narrow ditches. The bank was the metalled way and the ditches served for drainage. Small holes along the roadside are the remains of the stone quarries from which they obtained the road-building material.

Hollow ways usually mean that the sites of fields, villages or farms are close by. On the hill slopes, ancient fields appear as terraces divided by the baulks of unploughed land, which run parallel to the contours of the slopes, and they may be either the square fields of the early Celts, which were in use from the late Bronze Age, and lingered on in some places into late Roman times, or the long narrow fields of the Belgae, which were used during the Iron Age and the Roman occupation and on through Anglo-Saxon and early medieval times.

A group of large craters in chalky downland is probably the site of Neolithic and Bronze Age flint mines, while deep trenches in metal-bearing areas may be the sites of open-cast mining for copper, silver or lead: and if so, nearby patches of ground which are markedly bare of vegetation could be the sites of ancient slag heaps.

To become familiar with flints, it is best to try your hand at making them yourself. After all, prehistoric man managed it, with nothing but his two hands. Flint usually occurs in large nodules in chalk and certain limestones, sometimes lying strewn over the ground.

Flint easily fractures when struck, producing a usefully sharp cutting edge, for it breaks not in irregular lumps or along flat surfaces but in gently curving ripples, giving a shell-like fracture. Both the core and the flakes struck from it can be further trimmed to make the variety of tools of the Stone Age, the hand-axes, scrapers, knives, arrowheads and gravers.

For retouching these implements pressure can be applied instead of percussion, thereby producing the long shallow flakes from which the beautiful Solutrean leaf-shaped spear and arrow heads were made.

Obsidian, which is a natural form of volcanic glass, and

crystalline rocks can be struck and pressured in the same way as flint, but to produce an effective cutting edge the implements of crystalline rock must be sharpened by grinding and polishing. Towards the end of the Stone Age implements of flint were also ground and polished in this way. The commonest implements of ground stone are 'celts'—axe-heads, adze blades, chisels or gouges.

Stone-axes and arrowheads were mostly fixed to wooden shafts by lashing with fibre and applying gum for added strength, but sometimes the celt, by patient boring, was perforated, and the haft inserted in the hole.

When finds turn up on a dig their careful recording is vital. The record for each object found must include its exact provenance, with the number of the level, its size, colour, the material of which it is made and, where possible, its purpose; and only at times of blank bafflement should you resort to the despairing description, first attributed to that great archaeologist, Sir Flinders Petrie: "loom weight, net sinker, spindle whorl or whatnot"—although even this is better than the comment of Samuel Pepys, when he looked for the first time on the ruins of Stonehenge: "God knows what their use was!"

Chronological Tables

THE ICE AGE

	Began	Ended	
1st Glacial (Günz)	1 million to 660,000 years ago	560,000	
1st Interglacial	560,000	460,000	Australopithecus Pithecanthropus Erectus Pekin Man (Sinanthropus)
2nd Glacial (Mindel)	460,000	420,000	
2nd Interglacial	420,000	220,000	
3rd Glacial (Riss)	220,000	180,000	Neanderthal Man
3rd Interglacial	180,000	80,000	
4th Glacial (Würm)	80,000	10,000	Homo Sapiens

BRITAIN

Palaeolithic period	began	about	500,000 B.C.
Mesolithic	began	about	12,000 to 10,000 B.C.
Separation of Britain from Mainland of Europe		about	8000 B.C.
Neolithic	began	about	4000 B.C.
Bronze Age	began	about	2000 B.C.
Iron Age	began	about	500 B.C.
Roman Conquest			A.D. 43

Book List

Burkitt, M. C., *Our Early Ancestors*, Camb. U.P. 1926.

Burkitt, M. C., *South Africa's Past In Stone And Paint*, Camb. U.P. 1928.

Carrington, Richard, *A Guide to Earth History*, Chatto and Windus, 1959.

Childe, V. Gordon, *A Short Introduction To Archaeology*, Methuen, 1956.

Childe, V. Gordon, *What Happened In History*, Max Parrish, 1960.

Childe, V. Gordon, *The Prehistory of European Society*, Cassell, 1962.

Clark, Graham, *World Prehistory*, Camb. U.P. 1961.

Daniel, Glyn, *The First Civilisations*, Pelican, 1968.

Dawson, Christopher, *The Age of The Gods*, John Murray, 1928.

Hawkes, C. and J., *Prehistoric Britain*, Pelican, 1953.

Hawkes, J., *A Guide to the Prehistoric and Roman Monuments in England and Wales*, Chatto and Windus, 1951.

Hawkes, J., *Early Britain*, Collins, 1945.

Merrifield, Ralph, *Roman London*, Cassell, 1969.

Pendlebury, J. D. S., *The Archaeology of Crete*, Methuen, 1939.

Piggott, Stuart, *The Neolithic Cultures of the British Isles*, Camb. U.P. 1954.

Piggott, Stuart, *Ancient Europe*, Edin. U.P. 1965.

Smith, G. Elliot, *Human History*, Jonathan Cape, 1933.

Webster, Graham, *Practical Archaeology*, A. and C. Black, 1963.

Weigall, Arthur, *The Life and Times of Akhnaton*, Thornton Butterworth, 1922.

Weigall, Arthur, *A Short History of Ancient Egypt*, Chapman and Hall, 1939.

Woolley, Leonard, *The Excavations at Ur and the Hebrew Record*, Allen and Unwin, 1929.

Woolley, Leonard, *History Unearthed*, Benn, 1963.

Index

Index